hamlyn
QuickCook

hamlyn

QuickCook
Fish

Recipes by Emma Lewis

Every dish, three ways – you choose!
30 minutes | 20 minutes | 10 minutes

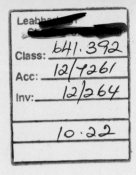
An Hachette UK Company
www.hachette.co.uk

First published in Great Britain in 2012 by Hamlyn,
a division of Octopus Publishing Group Ltd
Endeavour House, 189 Shaftesbury Avenue
London WC2H 8JY
www.octopusbooks.co.uk

Recipes by Emma Lewis

ISBN 978-0-60062-390-8

A CIP catalogue record for this book is available from the British Library

Printed and bound in China

10 9 8 7 6 5 4 3 2 1

Both metric and imperial measurements are given for the recipes. Use one set of
measures only, not a mixture of both.

Standard level spoon measurements are used in all recipes
1 tablespoon = 15 ml
1 teaspoon = 5 ml

Ovens should be preheated to the specified temperature. If using a fan-assisted oven,
follow the manufacturer's instructions for adjusting the time and temperature. Grills
should also be preheated.

This book includes dishes made with nuts and nut derivatives. It is advisable for
those with known allergic reactions to nuts and nut derivatives and those who may
be potentially vulnerable to these allergies, such as pregnant and nursing mothers,
invalids, the elderly, babies and children, to avoid dishes made with nuts and nut
oils. It is also prudent to check the labels of prepared ingredients for the possible
inclusion of nut derivatives.

The Department of Health advises that eggs should not be consumed raw. This book
contains some dishes made with raw or lightly cooked eggs. It is prudent for more
vulnerable people such as pregnant and nursing mothers, invalids, the elderly, babies
and young children to avoid uncooked or lightly cooked dishes made with eggs.

Contents

Introduction

30 20 10 – Quick, Quicker, Quickest

This book offers a new and flexible approach to meal-planning for busy cooks, letting you choose the recipe option that best fits the time you have available. Inside you will find 360 dishes that will inspire and motivate you to get cooking every day of the year. All the recipes take a maximum of 30 minutes to cook. Some take as little as 20 minutes and, amazingly, many take only 10 minutes. With a bit of preparation, you can easily try out one new recipe from this book each night and slowly you will be able to build a wide and exciting portfolio of recipes to suit your needs.

How Does it Work?

Every recipe in the QuickCook series can be cooked one of three ways – a 30-minute version, a 20-minute version or a super-quick and easy 10-minute version. At the beginning of each chapter you'll find recipes listed by time. Choose a dish based on how much time you have and turn to that page.

You'll find the main recipe in the middle of the page accompanied by a beautiful photograph, as well as two time-variation recipes below.

If you enjoy your chosen dish, why not go back and cook the other time-variation options at a later date? So if you've tried and liked the 20-minute Smoked Haddock and Corn Chowder, but only have 10 minutes to spare this time around, you'll find a way to cook the same flavours in a different recipe using cheat ingredients or clever shortcuts.

If you love the ingredients and flavours of the 10-minute Prosciutto, Scallop and Rosemary Skewers, why not try something more substantial, like the 20-minute Scallop, Chorizo and Rosemary Stew, or be inspired to make a more elaborate version, like the Scallops with Rosemary Risotto? Alternatively, browse through all 360 delicious recipes, find something that catches your eye – then cook the version that fits your time frame.

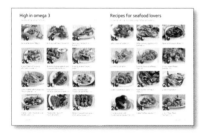

Or, for easy inspiration, turn to the gallery on pages 12–19 to get an instant overview by themes, such as High in Omega 3 or Recipes for Seafood Lovers.

QuickCook online

To make life even easier, you can use the special code on each recipe page to email yourself a recipe card for printing, or email a text-only shopping list to your phone. Go to www.hamlynquickcook.com and enter the recipe code at the bottom of each page.

FIS-FAMI-WEG

Fast Fish

With little time to spare, many of us are looking for easier ways to prepare a meal. It's tempting to reach for a takeaway menu or fast-forward to the 'ping' of a microwave, but these catering solutions often don't offer value for money, nor are they reliably nutritious. Home cooking wins on both these counts and yet it doesn't have to be elaborate or time-consuming, especially if you choose fish. As well as being very good for you, which is why we are all advised to eat it twice a week, fish is also super quick to cook. Many fish dishes take no longer than 10 minutes to rustle up – in fact, because of its delicate flesh, fish is at its best cooked briefly.

Tooling up

Anyone who likes cooking fish should invest in a large, heavy-based nonstick frying pan, which is perfect for cooking thin fish fillets in a flash. Chunkier fillets of firm-fleshed fish will benefit greatly from being cooked on a griddle pan, giving your fish an appealing smoky, barbecue-like taste. Poaching is a subtle and healthy way of cooking fish – choose a large, shallow pan for this method, which will also be suitable for steaming. For grilling and roasting fish, a large roasting tin is ideal for cooking several fish fillets in one go when you don't have much time, or for cooking a whole fish for a special occasion. If you can't resist a piece of deep-fried fish, make sure you have a large, deep saucepan to hold enough oil for deep-frying, and a thermometer is also useful for checking the temperature.

Stocking up

Fish has a wonderful, delicate flavour all of its own. You can serve it really simply with just a squeeze of lemon juice or top it off with some fresh herbs and a little butter. But it also tastes good teamed with punchy flavours, so keep jars of olives, capers and cornichons in your kitchen cupboard for an instant piquant accompaniment or stir them through some mayonnaise for an easy condiment. Chunkier sauces like pesto and salsa also go well with fish, while a handful of breadcrumbs scattered over and crisped up as a topping is especially inviting for kids. You can't store fresh fish for very long, but canned fish is invaluable to have around. Tuna is a firm favourite for most families and, like canned salmon, is endlessly versatile

– try it stirred into pasta, made into a fishcake or simply served as salad. Anchovies won't satisfy the appetite, but a couple of them added to a sauce or dressing will immediately bring a richness to the flavour. Fish can be frozen, but the texture does suffer in the process. Seafood, however, is fine for freezing – prawns, for example, make a wonderful last-minute meal cooked with frozen peas in a risotto, and squid and scallops are also worthy candidates for the freezer.

Shopping for fish

Fish is widely available in supermarkets these days, and many of the larger stores have dedicated fish counters offering a great selection of fresh produce. You may also be fortunate enough to have a fishmonger nearby. It's worth tracking down one of these gems, as the staff are so knowledgeable about the different types of fish on offer, and are able to expertly clean, fillet and present it as well as provide you with plenty of tips on cooking. They can also talk you through the issues of fish sustainability – as our enjoyment of fish has increased, a number of species have been over-fished and are now protected. Seafood can be quite expensive, and turbot or lobster is probably best enjoyed as a special treat. But with a little shopping around, you'll find fish that's affordable enough to be eaten everyday. Try using relatively inexpensive gurnard or coley in place of pricier cod and haddock, while rainbow trout is a dependable all-round fish and salmon can be a surprising bargain. Mackerel and sardines are not only packed full of essential oils and vitamins, they are also really cost-effective choices. If you like seafood, prawns are often good value and a few of the larger variety go a long way, while clams and mussels are often cheaper than you might expect.

Choosing the right fish

People are often a bit squeamish about buying fish and worried about how to choose the freshest possible. You can tell a lot from the appearance of a fish – look for bright, fresh eyes and a clear skin. Fillets and steaks should also have clear-coloured skin, be firm to the touch (not breaking apart) and, contrary to what some might think, no fish should smell fishy when it's bought. The classic smell that can put people off eating fish comes from decomposition, so any fishy fish are best avoided! It's sometimes a little overwhelming looking at a fish counter offering a wide selection of fish. Where do you start if you've never cooked fish before? What will all the family enjoy eating? What will make a really impressive dinner? The following guide will help you to understand the different types of fish available.

Classic white fish

Flaky white fish such as cod, haddock, hake, coley, pollack and whiting are the most popular options. They don't have an overpowering taste, are low in fat and make a safe choice if you are unsure about eating fish. You can interchange any of these fish in the recipes in this book, depending on what is available in the shops and your budget. They are quick to cook and very versatile – you'll find nice thick fillets, or chunky steaks that are great to cook speedily under the grill or that can be sliced into thin strips and added to a stew or stir-fry for super-fast meals. Just make sure you don't cook the fish too long, or it will break apart into flakes.

Dependable salmon and tuna

For those who think they don't like fish, or would prefer to eat meat, robust and flavourful salmon and tuna are your best options. Salmon is probably the most versatile fish of all – you can prepare and cook salmon steaks or fillets in a wide variety of ways, or cut it into chunks for stews, mince it for a child-friendly dish or serve up a whole salmon for entertaining. Fresh tuna is normally sold as steaks and needs only the briefest of cooking – like a fine beef steak, the centre should be ruby rare, so literally a minute or two under the grill is all it needs. Salmon should be cooked through but again doesn't need long or it will lose its natural moistness.

Fish packed full of essential oils

To reduce the risk of heart disease, it's recommended that we eat at least one portion of oily fish a week to reap the benefits of all the healthy fish oils. Salmon is packed full of these oils, as is fresh (but not canned) tuna. But you might also like to try mackerel, which has lots of flavour and is great in a curry, the smaller sardine or that Scandinavian favourite the herring.

Something a bit more adventurous

More uncommon and a little higher in price are white fish such as sea bass, red mullet and sea bream. These fish are a real treat when cooked whole but are also good if you are short on time cut into fillets and served with a flavourful sauce. For something sturdier in texture, look out for monkfish, which has a dense, sweet flesh that some people liken to lobster. The robust flesh of swordfish makes it the perfect choice for threading on to skewers to cook on the barbecue. Halibut, which comes in enormous steaks, is another foolproof firm fish and is great in a curry. Squid and scallops take just a minute or so to cook and will give any dish the wow factor. Their flesh is tough enough to stand up to some feisty cooking methods – they are both well-suited to being deep-fried or stewed – but their delicate yet distinctive flavours also lend themselves to being quickly fried and then just served with a wedge of lemon for squeezing over. There are many more exotic fish available from fisheries around the world – among these, hoki, red snapper and tilapia are all tasty white fish that you will come across from time to time and are well worth sampling.

Fish to impress

A whole fish presented on a serving platter is guaranteed to impress for a special meal. Flatfish tend to fall apart when stewed, so are best cut into fillets and simply cooked or left whole. Turbot and Dover sole are the kings of this type of fish and are much admired by chefs, but for something just a bit out of the ordinary for a weekday, try plaice or sole. Once thought of as the ultimate luxury, some shellfish and crustaceans can now be bought for surprisingly little and you often need only a relatively small amount to make an impact. Prawns are widely available, don't cost a fortune and are good for freezing. Look out for larger plump varieties, and for maximum flavour, keep the shell on. Langoustine, crab and lobsters are for special occasions only, but their plump sweet flesh makes a truly memorable treat. Clams and mussels are ideal for entertaining on a budget – they look slightly unusual but are simple to cook and great value for money.

12 Ways With Salmon

Deliciously different recipes for salmon-lovers

Corn Cakes with Smoked Salmon 52

Honey Mustard Salmon 82

Proper Salmon Fishcakes with Dill Sauce 84

Salmon Tikka Masala 90

Crispy Salmon and Pesto Parcels 98

Salmon, Pea and Dill Tortilla 106

Smoked Salmon Sushi Salad 194

Roasted Salmon with Peach Salsa 216

Crispy Rice Paper Salmon Parcels with Soy Dressing 234

Smoked Salmon and Beet Salad with Creamy Dressing 244

Confit Salmon with Watercress Salad 248

Hot-Smoked Salmon Kedgeree with Quails' Eggs 258

Pasta, Noodles and Rice

Filling recipes with a fish twist

Smoked Trout Pasta with
Creamy Dill Sauce 44

Seafood Risotto 62

Simple Tuna Pasta 110

Salmon and Leek Cannelloni
118

New Orleans Jambalaya 120

Prawn Laksa 132

Seafood Paella 134

Leek and Smoked Haddock
Risotto 142

Pad Thai 172

Tuna Soba Noodles with
Ponzu Dressing 186

Creamy Seafood Lasagne 260

Clam Linguine in Chilli
Crème Fraîche Sauce 276

Soups, Stews and Pot Pies

Easy recipes for winter days

Chinese Crab and Sweetcorn Soup 34

Trout and Bacon Hash 80

Smoked Haddock and Corn Chowder 86

Fish Pie 114

Spicy Peanut and Fish Stew 148

Monkfish, Chorizo and Chickpea Stew 156

Asian Fishball Soup 220

Bouillabaisse 232

Shellfish and Tomato Bisque 278

Tomato and Fennel Fish Pie 196

Smoked Haddock Soufflé 240

Prawn and Leek Pot Pies 254

Using the Whole Fish

Meals using whole fish that are sure to impress

Plaice Florentine 108

Lemon and Bacon-Wrapped Trout 146

Skate with Lemon Butter and Capers 150

Baked Sea Bream with Fennel 152

Baked Sea Bass with Romseco Salad 158

Sea Bream with Tomatoes and Basil 192

Couscous and White Fish Parcels 218

Chinese Banquet Sea Bass 246

Baked Turbot with a Buttery Tarragon Sauce 256

Whole Roasted Salmon with Lemon and Herb Tartare 264

Pan-Fried Dover Sole with Butter and Lemon 266

Sea Bass Baked in Salt Crust with Fennel Mayo 272

High in Omega 3

Healthy dishes for all the family

Smoked Mackerel Pâté 32

Anchovy and Olive Crostini 38

Moroccan Sardine Pitta Breads 48

Kipper Salad with Creamy Mustard Dressing 54

Mackerel Goujons with Soured Cream and Paprika Dip 64

Crunchy Sardine Caesar Salad 92

Baked Mullet with Orange and Olive Couscous 128

Mackerel with Roasted Tomatoes and Horseradish 138

Halibut Ceviche with Grapefruit and Chillies 198

Smoked Trout, Cucumber and Radish Salad 206

Oatmeal Herrings with Beetroot Salad 212

Grilled Mackerel with Lemon, Chilli and Coriander 226

Recipes for Seafood Lovers

A selection of original recipes using shellfish and seafood

Italian Seafood Salad 24

Grilled Lemony Oysters with Spinach 40

Steamed Mussels in Wine 50

Crayfish Cocktail 56

Garlicky Prawn and Sherry Tapas 66

Crispy Lemon Prawn Skewers 102

Clams in Black Bean Sauce 140

Fruits de Mer with Herb Aioli 242

Lobster Thermidor 262

Creamy Oysters and Mushrooms in Brioche Pots 268

Citrus Scallop Ceviche 270

Crispy Deep-Fried Seafood 274

Touch of Spice

Enjoy a taste of the East with these hot and spicy recipes

Salt and Pepper Squid Bites 46

Spicy Tuna Empanadas 88

Fish Tortillas with Avocado Salsa 112

Cajun-Blackened Fish Steaks 136

Hake with Spicy Coriander Pesto 144

Tuna Teriyaki with Wasabi Mash 154

Peppered Tuna with Rocket and Parmesan 170

Steamed Sea Bream with Asian Flavours 180

Coconut Fish Curry 208

Spiced Fish Tagine 224

Crab Cakes with Chipotle Salsa 238

Chilli Crab 252

Comfort Food

Indulge yourself with these comforting fish-flavoured treats

Vietnamese Spring Rolls 28

Indian Prawn Omelette Wraps 58

Best-Ever Crab Sandwich 68

Mini Garlicky Cod Bites 70

Beer-Battered Cod and Chips 76

Asian Seafood Noodles 78

Mini Seafood Pizza Bites 94

Sweet and Sour Fish 100

Smoked Haddock Rarebit 122

Tuna Burgers with Mango Salsa 182

Healthy Fish Supper with Homemade Tomato Ketchup 190

Oven-Baked Thai Fishcakes 202

QuickCook
Light
Bites

Recipes listed by cooking time

10

2⏱ Italian Seafood Salad

Serves 4

150 ml (¼ pint) dry white wine
1 shallot, finely chopped
500 g (1 lb) cleaned live clams
150 g (5 oz) raw peeled large
    prawns
6 cleaned large scallops
1 lemon
handful of basil, chopped
5 tablespoons extra virgin olive oil
100 g (3½ oz) cherry tomatoes,
    halved
100 g (3½ oz) salad leaves
salt and pepper

• Bring the wine and shallot to the boil in a saucepan. Reduce the heat and add the clams. Cover the pan and cook for 5 minutes until the clams have opened. Discard any that remain closed. Remove from pan with a slotted spoon and leave to cool.

• Add the prawns to the pan and cook for 1–2 minutes. Add the scallops and cook for a further 3 minutes, turning halfway through cooking, until the prawns are pink and just cooked through. Set the prawns to one side and slice the scallops.

• Whisk together the finely grated rind of the lemon with a good squeeze of the juice, the basil, oil and a little of the seafood cooking liquid. Season and then toss the seafood in half the dressing.

• Arrange the tomatoes and salad leaves on serving plates. Place the seafood on top and spoon over the remaining dressing to serve.

1⏱ Spicy Seafood Salad

Cook 100 g (3½ oz) raw squid rings in hot water for 2 minutes. Drain and cool. Mix together 1 crushed garlic clove, 1 finely chopped red chilli, 1 tablespoon fish sauce, a pinch of caster sugar and a squeeze of lime juice. Toss with 125 g (4 oz) cooked peeled large prawns, the squid, ¼ sliced cucumber, 1 sliced Cos lettuce and a large handful of coriander and mint, chopped.

3⏱ Seafood Pancakes with Basil Sauce

Cook the seafood as above. Boil the cooking liquid until reduced to 50 ml (2 fl oz). Stir in 100 ml (3½ fl oz) single cream, a good squeeze of lemon juice and a handful of basil, chopped. Keep warm. Meanwhile, place 125 g (4 oz) plain flour in a bowl. Crack in 2 eggs, mix together, then slowly beat in 300 ml (½ pint) milk. Season. Heat a little olive oil in a nonstick frying pan.

Cook a ladleful of the batter for 30 seconds. Turn over and cook for 30 seconds more until just cooked through. Keep warm. Repeat to make 6–8 pancakes. Stir the seafood into the sauce. Use to fill the pancakes. Top with a little of the sauce and extra chopped herbs.

Prosciutto, Scallop and Rosemary Skewers

Serves 3–4

6 thin slices of prosciutto
12 cleaned large scallops
12 long, thick rosemary sprigs
3 tablespoons olive oil
salt

- Cut the prosciutto in half lengthways. Wrap a piece around each scallop.

- Strip the leaves from the bottom of each rosemary sprig, then thread each scallop on to a rosemary 'skewer'.

- Drizzle over the oil and season with salt. Cook under a hot grill or on a hot barbecue for 5 minutes, or until just cooked through, turning once.

Scallop, Chorizo and Rosemary

Stew Heat 1 tablespoon olive oil in a large saucepan. Cook 125 g (4 oz) chorizo, cut into thick slices, for about 2 minutes until golden. Add 2 sliced garlic cloves and cook for 30 seconds. Stir in 1 teaspoon tomato purée followed by 100 ml (3½ fl oz) dry white wine and cook until nearly boiled away. Pour over a 400 g (13 oz) can chopped tomatoes and a rosemary sprig. Bring to the boil, then simmer for 8 minutes, adding a little water if necessary. Stir in 12 cleaned plump scallops and cook for 2–3 minutes until just cooked through. Scatter over a handful of chopped flat leaf parsley just before serving.

Scallops with Rosemary Risotto

Heat 1 tablespoon olive oil in a deep frying pan. Add 1 chopped onion and cook for 5 minutes until softened, then add 1 crushed garlic clove and cook for a further 1 minute. Stir in 300 g (10 oz) risotto rice until well coated. Pour in 75 ml (3 fl oz) dry white wine and 1 teaspoon finely chopped rosemary and boil until the wine has reduced. Add about 1.2 litres (2 pints) hot vegetable stock, a ladleful at a time, stirring and simmering after each addition until the stock is absorbed before adding the next. Continue until all the stock is absorbed and the rice is tender, about 15–18 minutes. Dot with 25 g (1 oz) butter, cover and leave to stand for 2 minutes. Meanwhile, heat 1 tablespoon olive oil in a frying pan. Cook 4 prosciutto strips for 1 minute on each side until crisp. Remove from the pan. Add 8 cleaned scallops and cook for 2 minutes on each side until golden. Top the risotto with the scallops and crumble over the prosciutto to serve.

30 Seared Tuna with Niçoise Salad

Serves 4

300 g (10 oz) salad potatoes, halved
2 eggs
100 g (3½ oz) green beans
1 tablespoon olive oil
450 g (14½ oz) piece of very fresh tuna
125 g (4 oz) cherry tomatoes, halved
2 Cos lettuces
8 anchovy fillets in oil, drained
75 g (3 oz) black olives
salt and pepper

For the vinaigrette

2 garlic cloves, crushed
1 teaspoon Dijon mustard
1 tablespoon red wine vinegar
1 tablespoon lemon juice
6 tablespoons extra virgin olive oil
handful of parsley, chopped

· Cook the potatoes in a saucepan of lightly salted boiling water for 12–15 minutes until just tender. Drain and cool under cold running water. Meanwhile, gently lower the eggs into a saucepan of boiling water and cook for 8 minutes. Drain and cool as before, then shell. Cook the beans in a saucepan of salted boiling water for 5 minutes until just tender. Drain and cool as before.

· Meanwhile, mix together all the ingredients for the vinaigrette and season well. Toss half the vinaigrette with the potatoes and beans and set aside. Rub the oil over the tuna and season well. Heat a griddle pan until smoking hot and cook for 2 minutes on each side until browned but still rare inside. Cut into bite-sized pieces.

· Toss the tomatoes with the potatoes and beans. Separate the leaves of the lettuces, then arrange on a serving plate with the anchovies, olives, eggs, quartered, the tuna slices and drizzle over the remaining dressing.

1 **Niçoise Sandwich**
Mix together 100 g (3½ oz) drained canned tuna in oil, 1 crushed garlic clove, 1 crushed anchovy fillet and 4 tablespoons mayonnaise. Spread over 2 slices of bread. Top with a handful of sun-dried tomatoes, chopped, and some rocket leaves, then cover each with another slice of bread. Cut in half to serve.

2 **Easy Niçoise with Vinaigrette**
Cook 2 eggs in boiling water for 8 minutes. Drain and cool under the cold tap, then shell. Meanwhile, cook 100 g (3½ oz) green beans in lightly salted boiling water for 5 minutes. Drain and cool. Toss the beans with 125 g (4 oz) cherry tomatoes, 100 g (3½ oz) chargrilled artichokes from a jar and

75 g (3 oz) black olives. Prepare the vinaigrette as above, adding 4 crushed anchovy fillets. Stir a little through the bean mixture with a drained 200 g (7 oz) can tuna in oil. Arrange the leaves of 2 Cos lettuces on a plate. Top with the tuna mixture and quartered eggs. Drizzle with the remaining dressing to serve.

 # Smoked Mackerel Pâté

Serves 4

250 g (8 oz) smoked mackerel
  fillets
1 lemon
200 g (7 oz) cream cheese
handful of flat leaf parsley and
  chives, chopped, plus extra
  to serve
salt and pepper
Melba toasts, to serve

- Discard the skin and any bones from the fish. Finely grate the rind of about half the lemon.

- Place the fish and lemon rind in a food processor with the cream cheese and pulse until just combined. Season well with pepper, add salt and juice from the lemon to taste and stir through the herbs.

- Place in serving bowls, sprinkle with more herbs and serve with Melba toasts.

 ### Mackerel with Bacon Sauce

Place 1 large gutted mackerel on a lightly greased baking sheet. Dot with butter. Place in a preheated oven, 200°C (400°F), Gas Mark 6, for 15 minutes. Meanwhile, cut 3 streaky bacon rashers into matchsticks. Cook in a little olive oil in a saucepan until crisp. Remove. Add 1 chopped shallot and cook for 3 minutes. Add 1 crushed garlic clove and cook for 30 seconds. Add 50 ml (2 fl oz) dry white wine. Boil until reduced by half. Return the bacon and pour over 75 ml (3 fl oz) water. Cook for 2 minutes. Stir in 4 tablespoons crème fraîche. Heat through. Spoon over the mackerel. Scatter with chopped flat leaf parsley.

 ### Creamy Mackerel and Potato Bake

Cook 3 peeled and halved potatoes in a saucepan of lightly salted boiling water for 10–15 minutes until just cooked through. Drain, then slice as thinly as you can. Meanwhile, heat 25 g (1 oz) butter in a saucepan. Add 1 chopped onion and cook for 5 minutes until softened. Stir in 100 ml (3½ fl oz) double cream. Discard the skin and any bones from 2 x 150 g (5 oz) smoked mackerel fillets, then break into flakes. Stir through the sauce with 1 teaspoon wholegrain mustard. Mix with the potato slices and place in a lightly greased baking dish. Scatter over 50 g (2 oz) dried breadcrumbs and drizzle with olive oil. Cook under a preheated hot grill for 5–10 minutes until bubbling and golden. Serve immediately with a green salad.

Chinese Crab and Sweetcorn Soup

Serves 4

3 corn cobs
1.2 litres (2 pints) chicken stock
1 tablespoon Shaoxing wine
1 tablespoon soy sauce
2 teaspoons finely chopped fresh root ginger
2 teaspoons cornflour
1 tablespoon water
200 g (7 oz) white crabmeat
1 egg, beaten
2 spring onions, chopped
salt and pepper

- Use a sharp knife to cut the kernels from the corn cobs. Place both the kernels and the cobs in a saucepan with the stock and simmer for 12 minutes. Discard the cobs. Scoop out half the kernels and set aside. Purée the remainder with a stick blender until creamy.

- Return the whole kernels to the pan along with the Shaoxing wine, soy sauce and ginger. Mix the cornflour with the measurement water and stir into the soup along with the crabmeat. Simmer until heated through and slightly thickened. Season to taste.

- Stirring the soup with a large spoon, slowly pour in the egg in one long stream to create silky strands of egg through the soup. Scatter over the spring onions and serve.

 Crab and Sweetcorn Bites

Mix together 150 g (5 oz) drained canned white crabmeat, 100 g (3½ oz) drained canned sweetcorn kernels, 1 sliced spring onion, 1 tablespoon self-raising flour and 1 beaten egg. Heat 1 tablespoon vegetable oil in a nonstick frying pan and drop large separate spoonfuls of the mixture into the pan. Cook for 2–3 minutes on each side until golden.

 Sweetcorn Risotto with Crab

Heat 1 tablespoon olive oil and 1 tablespoon butter in a large saucepan. Cook 1 finely chopped onion for 5 minutes until softened. Stir in 300 g (10 oz) risotto rice until well coated. Pour in 50 ml (2 fl oz) dry white wine and cook until nearly boiled away. Add about 1 litre (1¾ pints) vegetable stock, a ladleful at a time, stirring and simmering after each addition until the stock is absorbed before adding the next. Meanwhile, cook 100 g (3½ oz) fresh sweetcorn kernels in boiling water for 5 minutes until soft. Drain, then whizz in a food processor with 5 tablespoons crème fraîche until smooth. After 15 minutes of cooking the risotto when all the stock is absorbed and the rice is nearly cooked through, add the puréed sweetcorn and cook for a few minutes more until the rice is tender. Stir in 150 g (5 oz) white crabmeat. Top with dollops of crème fraîche and some chopped chives to serve.

30 Baked Eggs with Smoked Fish and Leeks

Serves 4

150 ml (¼ pint) milk
250 g (8 oz) smoked haddock fillet
25 g (1 oz) butter
2 small leeks, thinly sliced
1 tablespoon plain flour
3 tablespoons crème fraîche
4 eggs
salt and pepper
toasted brown bread, to serve

- Pour the milk over the haddock in a shallow saucepan. Simmer for 7–10 minutes until the fish flakes easily. Strain the milk through a sieve into a jug. When the fish is cool enough to handle, tear into flakes, discarding the skin and any bones.

- Meanwhile, melt half the butter in a saucepan. Add the leeks and a splash of water and cook for 5 minutes until soft. Stir in the flour and cook for 2 minutes. Slowly whisk in the poaching milk until smooth. Bring to the boil, whisking, then simmer for a few minutes until slightly thickened. Season well. Stir in the crème fraîche.

- Divide the leek mixture between 4 individual ramekins or ovenproof dishes on a baking sheet. Arrange the haddock on top. Crack an egg into each and dot with the remaining butter. Place in a preheated oven, 180°C (350°F), Gas Mark 4, and cook for 10–12 minutes until the white is set and the yolks are still soft. Serve with toasted brown bread.

---

 1 **Creamy Smoked Fish Scrambled Eggs**

Crack 5 eggs into a nonstick saucepan over a medium heat. Dot over 50 g (2 oz) crème fraîche and leave for 1–2 minutes. Stir once, then leave for 30 seconds more. Break A 125 g (4 oz) skinless smoked mackerel fillet into small flakes, discarding any bones. Gently stir into the eggs. When the eggs are just setting but still creamy and moist, sprinkle over some chopped chives. Serve immediately on toasted brown bread.

 2 **Puffed Smoked Fish Omelette**

Pour 150 ml (¼ pint) milk over 250 g (8 oz) smoked haddock fillet in a shallow pan. Gently cook for 7–10 minutes until cooked through. Drain. When the fish is cool enough to handle, tear into flakes, discarding the skin and any bones. Meanwhile, separate 4 eggs. Lightly mix together the egg yolks with plenty of seasoning. Carefully whisk the egg whites in a grease-free bowl until just stiff. Stir one-third of the whites into the yolks, then carefully add the remainder in 2 batches. Heat 15 g (½ oz) butter in a nonstick frying pan. Add the egg mixture and cook for 1 minute. Scatter over the smoked haddock. Place the pan under a preheated medium grill, making sure you turn the handle away from the heat if not flameproof, and cook for a further 5 minutes, or until puffed and just set. Scatter over 1 chopped spring onion and serve immediately.

10 Anchovy and Olive Crostini

Serves 4

½ baguette, thickly sliced
1 large garlic clove, peeled
4 tablespoons extra virgin olive oil
3 tomatoes, chopped
4 anchovy fillets in oil, drained
  and sliced
1 teaspoon drained capers
50 g (2 oz) pitted black olives,
  roughly chopped
handful of basil, chopped
salt and pepper

- Place the baguette slices on a large baking sheet. Toast under a hot grill for 3 minutes. Turn over and toast the other side for 3 minutes until golden and crisp.

- Rub a little of the garlic clove over each piece of toasted bread, then drizzle over 2 tablespoons of the oil.

- Mix together the remaining ingredients and season well. Spoon a little of the mixture over each piece of toasted bread and serve.

 Bread, Anchovy and Olive Salad

Cut ½ baguette into bite-sized pieces. Arrange on a baking sheet. Place in a preheated oven, 200°C (400°F), Gas Mark 6, for 12 minutes until just golden and crisp. Meanwhile, mash together 3 drained anchovy fillets in oil and 1 crushed garlic clove until smooth. Stir in 5 tablespoons extra virgin olive oil, 1 tablespoon red wine and a good pinch of chilli flakes. Toss together the bread and 5 chopped tomatoes, then drizzle over the anchovy dressing. Leave for 5 minutes, then stir through 50 g (2 oz) pitted black olives and a handful of rocket leaves.

 Onion, Anchovy and Olive Puffs

Heat 2 tablespoons olive oil in a frying pan. Add 2 thinly sliced large onions and gently cook for 10 minutes until soft and golden. Meanwhile, use a small dinner plate, about 7 cm (3 inches) in diameter, to cut out 4 rounds from 375 g (12 oz) ready-rolled puff pastry. Place on a baking sheet. Spoon 2 tablespoons shop-bought fresh tomato pasta sauce over each round. Spoon over the cooked onions. Arrange 2 drained anchovy fillets in oil on top of each round and scatter over 50 g (2 oz) pitted black olives, divided between the rounds. Place in a preheated oven, 200°C (400°F), Gas Mark 6, for 15 minutes, or until crisp and cooked through.

Grilled Lemony Oysters with Spinach

Serves 4

1 tablespoon olive oil

150 g (5 oz) spinach

100 g (3½ oz) butter

2 egg yolks

lemon juice, to taste

1 teaspoon Worcestershire sauce

pinch of cayenne

12 live oysters, opened but in the shell

salt and pepper

- Heat the oil in a large saucepan. Add the spinach and a splash of water and cook for 2 minutes until wilted. Drain, pressing out the liquid, and finely chop.

- Melt the butter in a small saucepan until bubbling but not browned. Set a small heatproof bowl over a saucepan of simmering water, ensuring that the bottom of the bowl doesn't touch the water. Add the egg yolks and a good squeeze of lemon juice and whisk together. Whisking continuously, very slowly start to add the melted butter. As the mixture starts to thicken, you can add the butter a little more quickly. When thickened, season and add more lemon juice to taste, the Worcestershire sauce and cayenne.

- Discard the flat top shell of each oyster. Place a little spinach in each shell and sprinkle with more cayenne. Sit the oysters on a baking sheet and spoon over the sauce. Cook under a hot grill for 1 minute until the sauce has lightly browned.

 Smoked Mussel and Spinach Pasta

Cook 400 g (13 oz) fresh fettuccine according to the pack instructions. When the pasta is just cooked, stir in 150 g (5 oz) spinach leaves, then drain immediately, reserving some of the cooking water, and return to the pan. Meanwhile, mix together 100 g (3½ oz) smoked mussels, 1 beaten egg and a squeeze of lemon juice. Stir the mussel mixture through the pasta, adding a little of the reserved cooking water to loosen if necessary, then serve.

 Oyster and Spinach Open Sandwich

Split 2 individual baguettes in half. Wrap in foil, then place in a preheated oven, 200°C (400°F), Gas Mark 6, for 15 minutes until crisp. Leave to cool for 5 minutes. Meanwhile, beat 1 egg. Mix in 12 shucked live oysters. Toss 100 g (3½ oz) polenta with ½ teaspoon cayenne. Let the excess egg drip away from the oysters, then toss them in the spiced polenta until coated. Fill a large, deep saucepan one-third full with vegetable oil and heat until a cube of bread browns in 15 seconds. Deep-fry the oysters in batches for 2–3 minutes until crisp and golden. Drain on kitchen paper. While the oysters are frying, roughly chop 75 g (3 oz) spinach, rocket and watercress salad. Mix a good squeeze of lemon juice into 4 tablespoons mayonnaise and spread on the baked baguette halves. Place the salad on top, then add the warm fried oysters.

30 Charred Tomato, Prawn and Feta Salad

Serves 4

200 g (7 oz) cherry tomatoes, halved

5 tablespoons olive oil, plus extra for oiling

handful of oregano leaves, chopped

1 teaspoon crushed fennel seeds

150 g (5 oz) cooked peeled large prawns, tails on

1 tablespoon balsamic vinegar

100 g (3½ oz) rocket leaves

75 g (3 oz) feta cheese, crumbled

salt and pepper

- Place the tomatoes on a lightly oiled baking sheet. Drizzle over the oil, season with salt and pepper, then sprinkle a little of the oregano and crushed fennel seeds over each tomato. Place in a preheated oven, 200°C (400°F), Gas Mark 6, and cook for 15–20 minutes until browned and slightly shrivelled. Leave to cool for a few minutes.

- Toss the juices from the baking sheet with the balsamic vinegar and prawns. Then arrange on a serving plate with the rocket and cooked tomatoes. Scatter over the feta and serve.

 Prawns with Sun-Dried Tomato Feta Dip Mash together 75 g (3 oz) cream cheese and 25 g (1 oz) feta cheese until smooth, then thin with a little milk. Stir in 3 chopped sun-dried tomatoes and a handful of basil, chopped. Arrange 200 g (7 oz) cooked large peeled prawns on a serving plate and serve with the dip.

 Prawn Pasta with Tomatoes and Feta Place 200 g (7 oz) halved cherry tomatoes on a lightly oiled baking sheet. Drizzle over 5 tablespoons olive oil, then sprinkle over a handful of oregano leaves, chopped, and 1 teaspoon crushed fennel seeds. Place in a preheated oven, 200°C (400°F), Gas Mark 6, for 15–18 minutes until browned and slightly shrivelled. Meanwhile, cook 325 g (11 oz) dried trofie pasta according to the pack instructions. Add 100 g (3½ oz) raw peeled large prawns for the last 3 minutes of cooking and cook until they turn pink. Drain, reserving some of the cooking water, and return to the pan. Crumble over 50 g (2 oz) feta cheese and a little of the reserved cooking water. Stir until you have a smooth sauce. Add the cooked tomatoes and then spoon into serving bowls. Chop 50 g (2 oz) rocket leaves and scatter over the pasta.

Smoked Trout Pasta with Creamy Dill Sauce

Serves 4

400 g (13 oz) fresh linguine
6 tablespoons crème fraîche
squeeze of lemon juice
handful of dill, finely chopped,
  plus extra to serve
2 skinless smoked trout fillets,
  about 125 g (4 oz) each
2 spring onions, chopped
salt and pepper

- Cook the linguine according to the pack instructions.

- Meanwhile, mix together the crème fraîche, lemon juice and dill to make a smooth sauce. Break the trout into bite-sized pieces.

- Drain the pasta, reserving a little of the cooking water. Return to the pan and stir through the sauce, trout and spring onions. Season well and add a little of the reserved cooking water to loosen. Serve immediately with extra dill scattered over.

Potato Rosti with Smoked Trout

Cook 2 peeled large floury potatoes in a saucepan of boiling water for 5 minutes. Cool under the cold tap and pat dry. Roughly grate, squeezing over a little lemon juice to prevent discoloration. Using your hands, squeeze out any excess liquid and form into small cake shapes. Dust with plain flour. Heat 1 tablespoon olive oil and 15 g (½ oz) butter in a nonstick frying pan. Add the potato cakes and cook for 3–5 minutes on each side until golden and cooked through. Spoon 1 teaspoon crème fraîche on to each rosti, top with a large flake of smoked trout and scatter over some finely chopped dill to serve.

Smoked Trout Eggs

Cook 4 eggs in a saucepan of boiling water for 6 minutes. Drain and cool under the cold tap, then shell. In a food processor, whizz together 200 g (7 oz) each skinless smoked trout fillets and skinless fresh salmon fillet, the finely grated rind of 1 lemon and a handful of dill, chopped, until you have a smooth paste. Lightly wet your hands, then divide the paste into 4 and wrap a layer around each egg so that it is entirely encased. Dip the eggs into 1 beaten egg, then roll in 100 g (3½ oz) dried breadcrumbs to coat. Fill a large, deep saucepan one-third full with vegetable oil and heat until a cube of bread browns in

20 seconds. Deep-fry the eggs, in batches if necessary to avoid overcrowding the pan and lowering the oil temperature, for 3–4 minutes until golden and crisp all over. Drain on kitchen paper and serve with lemon wedges for squeezing over.

20 Salt and Pepper Squid Bites

Serves 4–6

500 g (1 lb) cleaned squid
2 teaspoons peppercorns, crushed
1 teaspoon chilli flakes
2 teaspoons salt
100 g (3½ oz) plain flour
vegetable oil, for deep-frying
2 spring onions, cut into thick slices
1 red chilli, cut into thick strips
lemon wedges, to serve

- Cut each squid tube in half. Lay flat, inside up, and use a sharp knife to gently score a cross. Cut into bite-sized pieces, then pat dry with kitchen paper.

- Mix together the crushed peppercorns, chilli flakes, salt and flour. Toss the squid in the mixture.

- Fill a large, deep saucepan one-third full with oil and heat until a cube of bread browns in 15 seconds. Shake off the excess flour from a handful of squid and deep-fry for 2–3 minutes until just golden and crisp. Drain on kitchen paper. Keep warm in a low oven. Repeat with the remaining squid.

- Deep-fry the spring onions and chilli strips for 1–2 minutes, and use to garnish the squid. Serve with lemon wedges for squeezing over.

---

10 Stir-Fried Salt and Pepper Squid

Crush together 1 teaspoon salt, ½ teaspoon pepper and a pinch each of Chinese five-spice powder and chilli flakes. Cut 500 g (1 lb) cleaned squid into thick rings. Heat 1 tablespoon vegetable oil in a wok and stir-fry half the squid for 1 minute. Remove from wok, add another tablespoon of oil and stir-fry the remaining squid for 1 minute. Return the first batch of squid to the wok along with the salt mix and 1 sliced spring onion. Stir around the wok until the squid is well coated, then serve immediately.

30 Salt and Pepper Squid Bites with

Chilli Jam For the chilli jam, place 2 large tomatoes in a saucepan with 200 g (7 oz) caster sugar and 4 finely chopped red chillies. Add 50 ml (2 fl oz) cider vinegar, 1 tablespoon fish sauce and a squeeze of lime juice. Bring to the boil and let the mixture bubble until the sugar melts. Then simmer for 20 minutes until sticky and thickened. Meanwhile, prepare and deep-fry the squid as above. Serve hot with the chilli jam.

Moroccan Sardine Pitta Breads

Serves 4

2 sardines, about 100 g (3½ oz) each, boned and each cut into 2 fillets
1 teaspoon ground cumin
pinch of cayenne
pinch of plain flour
3 tablespoons olive oil
1 tablespoon finely chopped preserved lemon
handful of coriander, chopped
handful of flat leaf parsley, chopped
4 pitta breads
1 tomato, chopped
¼ cucumber, sliced
salt and pepper

- Pat the sardines dry with kitchen paper and season. Mix together the cumin, cayenne and flour. Dust the fish all over with the spice mixture.

- Heat 1 tablespoon of the oil in a large, nonstick frying pan. Cook the fish, skin-side down, for 5 minutes. Turn over and cook for a further 3 minutes until cooked through. Keep warm.

- Mix the remaining oil with the preserved lemon and herbs, then season well. Lightly toast the pitta breads.

- Fill the pitta breads with the fish, tomato and cucumber, then drizzle over the dressing to serve.

 Devilled Sardines on Toast

Toast 4 thick slices of country bread. Heat 200 g (7 oz) canned sardines in tomato sauce with ½ teaspoon ground cumin and a pinch of cayenne until warmed through. Spoon over the toast and scatter with 1 tablespoon each finely chopped onion and chopped flat leaf parsley to serve.

 Spiced Moroccan Sardine Curry

Heat 2 tablespoons olive oil in a large, deep frying pan. Cook 1 finely chopped onion for 5 minutes. Stir in 2 finely chopped garlic cloves and cook for 2 minutes. Add 1 teaspoon each ground cumin and ground coriander followed by 2 teaspoons tomato purée. Stir in a 400 g (13 oz) can chopped tomatoes and a little water. Leave to simmer for 10 minutes.

Meanwhile, in a food processor, whizz together 500 g (1 lb) skinless sardine fillets, 1 egg yolk, 1 teaspoon paprika, the finely grated rind of 1 lemon and a handful each of parsley and coriander until smooth. Lightly wet your hands, then roll into walnut-sized balls. Season, then carefully add the fishballs to the pan. Simmer for 7–10 minutes until cooked through. Scatter over some more herbs, if you like, and serve with steamed couscous.

Steamed Mussels in Wine

Serves 4

2 tablespoons olive oil
2 garlic cloves, sliced
1.5 kg (3 lb) cleaned live mussels
200 ml (7 fl oz) dry white wine
handful of flat leaf parsley,
   chopped
crusty bread, to serve

· Heat the oil in a large saucepan. Add the garlic and cook for 30 seconds until lightly golden. Add the mussels and wine.

· Cover the pan and cook for 5 minutes, shaking the pan occasionally, until the mussels have opened. Discard any that remain closed.

· Stir in the parsley, then serve with crusty bread.

2 Mussel and Bacon Pasta

Heat 2 tablespoons olive oil in a saucepan. Cook 2 streaky bacon rashers, cut into matchsticks, for 3–5 minutes until golden. Add 1 finely chopped shallot. Cook for 3 minutes. Stir in 2 sliced garlic cloves, 750 g (1½ lb) cleaned live mussels and 200 ml (7 fl oz) dry white wine. Cover and cook for 5–7 minutes until the mussels have opened. Discard any that remain closed. Meanwhile, cook 325 g (11 oz) dried spaghetti according to the pack instructions. Drain the pasta and return to the pan. Lift out the mussels and add to the pasta. Boil to reduce the mussel liquid, if necessary, then stir in 4 tablespoons crème fraîche. Toss with the pasta. Scatter with a handful of flat leaf parsley, chopped.

3 Crispy Baked Mussels

Heat 2 tablespoons olive oil in a large saucepan. Cook 2 sliced garlic cloves for 30 seconds until lightly golden. Add 1.5 kg (3 lb) cleaned live mussels and 200 ml (7 fl oz) dry white wine, then season with salt. Cover and cook for 4 minutes until the mussels are just starting to open. Strain, reserving the liquid. Leave to cool a little, then discard any mussels that remain closed. Discard one half-shell from each mussel, leaving the mussels inside the remaining half-shells. Arrange on a baking sheet. Boil the reserved liquid until reduced to 50 ml (2 fl oz). Stir in 100 ml (3½ fl oz) double cream and boil until reduced to 75 ml (3 fl oz). Stir through a handful of flat leaf parsley, chopped. Spoon a little of the sauce over each mussel in its half-shell. Carefully sprinkle each mussel with some dried breadcrumbs and top with a small knob of butter. Place in a preheated oven, 220 °C (425 °F), Gas Mark 7, for 5 minutes, or until golden and bubbling.

 Corn Cakes with Smoked Salmon

Serves 4

2 eggs, beaten

4 tablespoons milk

300 g (10 oz) canned sweetcorn kernels, drained

75 g (3 oz) self-raising flour

2 spring onions, sliced

2 tablespoons vegetable oil

150 g (5 oz) smoked salmon

4 tablespoons mascarpone cheese

salt and pepper

chopped chives, to garnish

- Beat together the eggs, milk, sweetcorn, flour and spring onions until you have a smooth batter. Season well.

- Heat 1 tablespoon of the oil in a large, nonstick frying pan. Add half the batter to the pan in separate spoonfuls to make 6 small pancakes. Cook for 2–3 minutes on each side until golden and cooked through. Set aside on kitchen paper while you cook the remaining batter.

- Pile the pancakes on to serving plates and arrange the smoked salmon and mascarpone on top. Scatter with the chives and serve.

 Simple Corn and Salmon Pasta

Cook 400 g (13 oz) fresh penne according to the pack instructions. Add 125 g (4 oz) frozen sweetcorn kernels for the last 1 minute of cooking. Drain and return to the pan. Stir in 5 tablespoons crème fraîche and 150 g (5 oz) smoked salmon, torn into strips. Scatter over a handful of chives, chopped, to serve.

 Cajun Salmon with Corn Salsa

Make a Cajun spice mix by stirring together 1 tablespoon salt, 2 teaspoons paprika, 1 teaspoon ground cumin, ½ teaspoon each dried oregano and basil and a good pinch each of cayenne and pepper. Set aside half for another time and mix the remainder with 1 crushed garlic clove and 2 tablespoons olive oil. Rub all over 4 x 175 g (6 oz) salmon steaks and leave to marinate for 10–15 minutes. Cook on a hot barbecue or a smoking hot griddle pan for 5–7 minutes on each side until charred and cooked through. Meanwhile, use a sharp knife to cut the kernels from 2 corn cobs. Heat 1 tablespoon vegetable oil in a frying pan and cook until golden. Leave to cool a little, then stir through 1 chopped tomato, a squeeze of lime juice and some chopped coriander before serving.

Crayfish Cocktail

Serves 4

5 tablespoons mayonnaise

2 tablespoons tomato ketchup

Tabasco sauce, to taste

lemon juice, to taste

300 g (10 oz) cooked peeled
   crayfish tails

2 Little Gem lettuces, leaves
   separated

2 small ripe avocado, stoned,
   peeled and sliced

salt and pepper

paprika, to garnish

- Mix together the mayonnaise and ketchup, add Tabasco and lemon juice to taste and season. Stir through the crayfish.

- Pile the lettuce leaves into serving bowls and top with the avocado. Spoon over the crayfish mixture. Sprinkle with some paprika to garnish.

---

2 Mexican-Style Seafood Cocktail

Place 150 g (5 oz) raw peeled prawns in a bowl. Pour over boiling water to cover and leave for 2 minutes. Add 150 g (5 oz) cleaned scallops, adding a little more boiling water, and leave for a further 3 minutes, then drain. Mix together 300 ml (½ pint) tomato juice, 1 tablespoon tomato ketchup, a good squeeze of lime juice and Tabasco sauce to taste. Stir together with the seafood and leave to stand for 10 minutes. Spoon into serving bowls. Top with 1 chopped avocado, 1 sliced spring onion and a handful of chopped coriander.

3 Prawns in Warm Cocktail Sauce

Melt 100 g (3½ oz) butter in a small saucepan until bubbling but not browned. Set a small heatproof bowl over a saucepan of simmering water, ensuring that the bottom of the bowl doesn't touch the water. Add 2 egg yolks and a good squeeze of lemon juice and whisk together. Whisking constantly, very slowly start to add the melted butter. As the mixture starts to thicken, you can add the remainder a little more quickly. When thickened, leave to cool a little, then stir in 2 teaspoons tomato purée and a handful of tarragon, chopped.

In a separate bowl, whisk 100 ml (3½ fl oz) whipping cream until soft peaks form. Stir into the sauce, season and add Tabasco sauce to taste. Stir in 325 g (11 oz) cooked peeled large prawns. Spoon into individual gratin dishes. Cook under a preheated hot grill for 3 minutes until lightly browned.

 Indian Prawn Omelette Wraps

Serves 4

3 tablespoons vegetable oil

1 onion, sliced

2 garlic cloves, crushed

1 teaspoon finely chopped fresh root ginger

½ teaspoon ground cumin

200 g (7 oz) small raw peeled prawns

2 tomatoes, chopped

4 eggs, beaten

1 teaspoon garam masala

1 green chilli, finely chopped

handful of coriander, chopped

salt and pepper

4 warmed chapattis, to serve

- Heat 1 tablespoon of the oil in a frying pan. Add the onion and cook for 5 minutes until softened, then add the garlic, ginger and cumin and cook for a further 1 minute. Stir in the prawns and cook for 3 minutes, then add the tomatoes and cook until the prawns are pink and cooked through.

- Mix together the eggs, garam masala and chilli and season well. Heat ½ tablespoon of the remaining oil in a small, nonstick frying pan. Add one-quarter of the egg mixture and swirl around the pan. Stir once, then leave to cook for 1–2 minutes until starting to set. Spoon over one-quarter of the tomato prawn mixture and top with a little coriander. Place on a warmed chapatti and fold in half. Repeat with the remaining ingredients.

 Spicy Scrambled Eggs with Prawns

Mix together 1 teaspoon curry paste and 3 tablespoons crème fraîche. Crack 4 eggs into a nonstick saucepan and dot with the crème fraîche mixture. Season and cook over a low heat for 3 minutes. When the mixture starts to set, add 50 g (2 oz) cooked peeled small prawns and cook, stirring occasionally and breaking up the egg yolks, until creamy and just cooked through. Scatter over a handful of coriander, chopped, and serve immediately.

 Indonesian Prawn and Egg Curry

Heat 1 tablespoon vegetable oil in a saucepan. Add 1 chopped onion, 3 crushed garlic cloves and 2 teaspoons finely chopped fresh root ginger or galangal and cook for 5 minutes until softened. Stir in 1 tablespoon rendang or Thai red curry paste and ½ teaspoon turmeric. Cook for 1 minute. Pour over 200 ml (7 fl oz) chicken stock and 250 ml (8 fl oz) coconut milk. Add 2 lemon grass stalks and 2 kaffir lime leaves. Leave to simmer for 10–15 minutes. Meanwhile, cook 4 eggs in a saucepan of boiling water for 8 minutes. Drain and cool under the cold tap, then shell. Stir 200 g (7 oz) raw peeled large prawns and the eggs into the curry. Simmer for 5 minutes, or until the prawns are pink or just cooked through. Scatter with chopped coriander.

1 Tuscan Tuna and Bean Salad

Serves 4

5 tablespoons mayonnaise

200 g (7 oz) can tuna in oil, drained

200 g (7 oz) canned cannellini beans, rinsed and drained

1 lemon

50 g (2 oz) rocket leaves

½ small red onion, finely chopped

1 tablespoon olive oil

salt and pepper

- Carefully mix the mayonnaise with the tuna and beans, taking care not to break the tuna up.

- Finely grate about half the rind of the lemon. Toss the rocket leaves and onion with the lemon rind. Whisk together the oil and a good squeeze of juice from the lemon, then season.

- Toss the rocket salad with the dressing, arrange in serving bowls and place the tuna and beans on top.

---

2 Tuna with Bean Mash

Cook 1 finely chopped small onion in 15 g (½ oz) butter in a saucepan for 5 minutes. Add 1 crushed garlic clove. Cook for 1 minute. Add 100 ml (3½ fl oz) single cream and 100 ml (3½ fl oz) stock. Bring to the boil. Add 2 x 400 g (13 oz) cans cannellini beans, rinsed and drained, and 1 thyme sprig. Simmer for 10 minutes. Discard the thyme and mash to a smooth paste. Meanwhile, brush 1 tablespoon olive oil over 4 x 150 g (5 oz) tuna steaks. Cook on a smoking hot griddle pan for 3 minutes on each side. Season well. Serve with the beans.

3 Tuna and Bean Pasta Bake

Cook 325 g (11 oz) dried penne according to the pack instructions. Add 200 g (7 oz) rinsed drained canned cannellini beans for the last 2 minutes of cooking. Drain and return to the pan. Meanwhile, melt 40 g (1½ oz) butter in a saucepan, stir in 40 g (1½ oz) plain flour and cook for 2 minutes. Slowly whisk in 500 ml (17 fl oz) milk until smooth. Bring to the boil, whisking, then simmer for a few minutes until thickened. Stir into the pasta and beans along with a drained 200 g (7 oz) can tuna in oil. Transfer to a baking dish. Mix together 50 g (2 oz) dried breadcrumbs and the finely grated rind of 1 lemon, then scatter over. Place in a preheated oven, 200°C (400°F), Gas Mark 6, for 15 minutes until crisp and browned.

30 Seafood Risotto

Serves 6

250 g (8 oz) mixed fish fillets,
such as sea bass, monkfish,
red mullet, cut into 2.5 cm
(1 inch) chunks

200 g (7 oz) raw small prawns,
shells on

1.5 litres (2½ pints) fish stock

150 ml (¼ pint) dry white wine

1 tablespoon olive oil

25 g (1 oz) butter

1 small onion, finely chopped

½ fennel bulb, finely chopped

500 g (1 lb) risotto rice

250 g (8 oz) cleaned live clams

100 g (3½ oz) raw squid rings

lemon juice, to taste

salt and pepper

- Place the fish and prawns in a large saucepan. Pour over the stock and wine and bring to the boil. Cook for 1–2 minutes until the seafood just turns opaque. Remove from the pan and set aside. Keep the stock simmering.

- Heat the oil with a little of the butter in a large saucepan. Add the onion and fennel and cook for 5 minutes. Stir in the rice until well coated. Add the hot stock, a ladleful at a time, stirring and simmering after each addition until the stock is absorbed before adding the next. After 15 minutes when the stock is absorbed and the rice is nearly cooked through, add the clams and cook for 3 minutes, then add the cooked seafood, squid rings and remaining butter. Season and squeeze over lemon juice to taste.

- Cover and leave to stand for 2 minutes. Discard any clams that remain closed, then serve.

1 Seafood Noodle Broth

Heat 1. 5 litres (2½ pints) stock, 2 fresh root ginger slices and 1 lemon grass stalk. Add 250 g (8 oz) cleaned live clams, 100 g (3½ oz) raw peeled prawns and 200 g (7 oz) dried fine rice noodles. Cook for 3 minutes. Add 75 g (3 oz) raw squid rings. Cook for 2 minutes or until all the seafood is cooked. Discard any clams that remain closed. Add some chopped coriander, then serve.

2 Seafood Rice

Cook 500 g (1 lb) white long-grain rice in a large saucepan of salted boiling water for 15 minutes until tender. Add 200 g (7 oz) frozen peas and 100 g (3½ oz) frozen raw squid rings for the last 3 minutes of cooking. Drain and return to the pan. Break 4 x 125 g (4 oz) skinless smoked mackerel fillets into large flakes, discarding any bones. Stir through the rice with 3 thinly sliced spring onions and a good squeeze of lemon juice. Scatter over plenty of chopped flat leaf parsley to serve.

Mackerel Goujons with Soured Cream and Paprika Dip

Serves 4

2 mackerel fillets, about 175 g
 (6 oz) each, cut into strips
75 g (3 oz) plain flour
1 egg, beaten
75 g (3 oz) dried breadcrumbs
2 garlic cloves, crushed
vegetable oil, for deep-frying
2 teaspoons smoked paprika
6 tablespoons soured cream
salt and pepper

- Pat the fish dry with kitchen paper. Dip into the flour followed by the egg. Mix together the breadcrumbs and garlic, then season well. Press the fish gently into the breadcrumb mixture until well coated.

- Fill a large, deep saucepan one-third full with oil and heat until a cube of bread browns in 15 seconds. Deep-fry the fish in batches for about 3 minutes until golden, crisp and cooked through. Drain on kitchen paper.

- Mix most of the paprika into the soured cream saving a pinch of paprika to sprinkle on top. Place in a small serving bowl and serve with the hot goujons.

 Simple Grilled Paprika Mackerel

Drizzle 2 tablespoons olive oil all over 4 x 175 g (6 oz) mackerel fillets and season. Cook, skin-side up, under a hot grill for 5 minutes. Turn over and cook for a further 3 minutes until just cooked through. Scatter over 2 finely chopped garlic cloves, 2 teaspoons smoked paprika and a small handful of flat leaf parsley, chopped, then serve with lemon wedges for squeezing over.

 Mackerel with Paprika Onion Crust Heat 2 tablespoons olive oil in a frying pan. Cook 1 sliced onion for 10 minutes until soft. Stir in 2 chopped garlic cloves and cook for a further 2 minutes. Place 2 x 175 g (6 oz) mackerel fillets on a baking sheet. Spoon over the onion and garlic. Mix together 50 g (2 oz) dried breadcrumbs, 1 tablespoon smoked paprika, the finely grated rind of 1 lemon and a handful of parsley, chopped. Scatter over the fish. Drizzle with a little more olive oil. Place in a preheated oven, 200°C (400°F), Gas Mark 6, for 15 minutes, or until crisp and the fish is cooked through.

 # Garlicky Prawn and Sherry Tapas

Serves 4

300 g (10 oz) raw large prawns,
tails on
2 tablespoons olive oil
2 garlic cloves, sliced
3 tablespoons fino or other
dry sherry
salt
handful of flat leaf parsley,
chopped, to garnish

· Heat the oil in a frying pan. Add the garlic followed by the prawns. Cook for 3 minutes, turning once, until golden. Pour over the sherry and let it bubble for 1–2 minutes. Season with salt, scatter over the parsley and serve immediately.

 ### Spanish Prawn and Sherry Stew

Heat 2 tablespoons olive oil in a saucepan and cook 3 sliced garlic cloves for 30 seconds until golden. Add a 400 g (13 oz) can chopped tomatoes, 3 tablespoons dry sherry and ½ teaspoon smoked paprika. Cook for 15 minutes. Meanwhile, cook 500 g (1 lb) salad potatoes in a saucepan of lightly salted boiling water for 12 minutes, or until tender. Drain and add to the stew along with 250 g (8 oz) raw peeled large prawns. Cook for a further 3–5 minutes until the prawns are cooked, then stir in 3 tablespoons crème fraîche. Serve with crusty bread.

 ### Prawn and Sherry Dim Sum

In a food processor, whizz together 250 g (8 oz) raw peeled prawns, 1 tablespoon dry sherry, 1 teaspoon sesame oil, ½ teaspoon finely chopped fresh root ginger, 1 crushed garlic clove and a pinch of caster sugar until smooth. Stir in 2 finely chopped spring onions. Lay out 16 round wonton wrappers and place a heaped teaspoon of the mixture on one half of each wrapper. Lightly wet your hands, then moisten the edge of each wrapper. Fold over each wrapper to form a half-moon shape, pressing with your thumb and forefinger to make little pleats and entirely enclose the filling. Heat 2 tablespoons vegetable oil in a nonstick frying pan. Fry the dumplings for 2–3 minutes until golden. Pour over 50 ml (2 fl oz) vegetable stock, cover and simmer/steam for 5–7 minutes until cooked through. Serve with soy sauce for dipping.

10 Best-Ever Crab Sandwich

Serves 2

25 g (1 oz) brown crabmeat
2 tablespoons mayonnaise
pinch of cayenne
1 teaspoon tomato ketchup
lemon juice, to taste
4 slices of crusty brown bread
75 g (3 oz) white crabmeat
salt and pepper
25 g (1 oz) watercress
lightly salted crisps, to serve
  (optional)

- Mix together the brown crabmeat, mayonnaise, cayenne and ketchup. Add lemon juice to taste and season.

- Spread the crab mixture over 2 slices of the bread. Scatter over the white crabmeat and watercress and top with the remaining slices of bread. Cut diagonally in half and serve with some lightly salted crisps, if you like.

20 Melting Crab Toasts

Mix together 2 sliced spring onions, 300 g (10 oz) white crabmeat and 5 tablespoons crème fraîche. Add a squeeze of lemon juice and a splash of Tabasco sauce, then season. Cut a baguette into thick slices. Toast under a preheated hot grill for 2–3 minutes on each side until starting to crisp. Remove and cool a little, leaving the grill on. Spread some of the crab mixture over each bread slice. Scatter over 25 g (1 oz) each grated Gruyère and Parmesan cheese. Cook under the grill for 3–5 minutes until bubbling and melted.

30 Crispy Crab Bites

Mix together 325 g (11 oz) brown and white crabmeat and 150 g (5 oz) cream cheese. Stir in a splash of Tabasco sauce and a squeeze of lemon juice, then season. Melt 50 g (2 oz) butter and mix with 3 tablespoons olive oil. Brush over 1 sheet of filo pastry, place another sheet of filo on top and brush again, then repeat once more so that you have 3 layers. Cut into 3 long strips, then cut each strip in half. Place a heaped teaspoon of the crab mixture at the bottom of each strip, fold over to make a triangle and keep folding to enclose the filling. Place on a baking sheet, brush over with the remaining oil mixture and place in a preheated oven, 200 °C (400 °F), Gas Mark 6, for 15 minutes until golden and crisp.

Mini Garlicky Cod Bites

Serves 4–6

40 g (1½ oz) butter, softened

2 garlic cloves, crushed

2 tablespoons finely grated Parmesan

handful of flat leaf parsley, chopped

500 g (1 lb) thick cod fillet, skinned

6 tablespoons olive oil, plus extra for oiling and drizzling

75 g (3 oz) dried breadcrumbs

salt and pepper

- Mix together the butter, garlic, Parmesan and parsley in a small bowl.

- Cut the cod into pieces about 2.5 cm (1 inch) thick, then season. Use a small, sharp knife to make a little pocket in the centre of each piece of fish. Push a small spoonful of butter inside each pocket. Close up the pockets so that no butter is visible.

- Place the oil and breadcrumbs on separate plates. Dip each piece of fish in the oil until really well coated, then roll in the breadcrumbs to coat. Place on an oiled baking sheet and drizzle over more oil. Place in a preheated oven, 200°C (400°F), Gas Mark 6, for 15 minutes until golden, crisp and cooked through.

 Lemon and Garlic Fried Cod

Cut 500 g (1 lb) thick cod fillet into pieces about 2.5 cm (1 inch) thick and dust with plain flour. Heat 1 tablespoon olive oil in a large, nonstick frying pan and cook the cod for 5 minutes, turning once, until golden and just cooked through. Add 1 sliced garlic clove to the pan along with 25 g (1 oz) butter and swirl around the pan. Cook for a further 1 minute, then squeeze over the juice of ½ lemon and scatter with chopped parsley.

Baked Cod with Garlicky Pesto Butter In a food processor, whizz together a large handful of basil, 2 crushed garlic cloves, 2 tablespoons grated Parmesan cheese and 1 tablespoon pine nuts until smooth. Add 50 g (2 oz) softened butter and pulse until well combined. Transfer the butter mixture to a sheet of foil, then roll it up in the foil into a cylinder and twist the ends to enclose. Chill in the freezer while you cook the cod. Place 4 x 175 g (6 oz) cod fillets on a lightly greased baking sheet. Place in a preheated oven, 200°C (400°F), Gas Mark 6, for 10 minutes. Unwrap the butter and cut into slices. Place a slice on top of each cod fillet and return to the oven for 2–3 minutes until the fish is cooked through and the butter has started to melt.

QuickCook
Family Meals

Recipes listed by cooking time

10

30 Beer-Battered Cod and Chips

Serves 4

25 g (1 oz) butter
2 spring onions, finely chopped
300 g (10 oz) frozen peas
150 g (5 oz) plain flour
350 ml (12 fl oz) beer
vegetable oil, for deep-frying
750 g (1½ lb) floury potatoes,
   peeled and cut into 1-cm
   (½-inch) thick chips
200 ml (7 fl oz) vegetable stock
4 cod fillets, about 175 g (6 oz)
   each, skin on
2 tablespoons cornflour
salt and pepper
lemon wedges, to serve

- Heat the butter in a small saucepan and cook the spring onions for 2 minutes until softened. Add the peas and stock and simmer for 3 minutes. Roughly mash and keep warm.

- Meanwhile beat together the flour and beer, then season well with salt and pepper.

- Fill a large, deep saucepan one-third full with oil and heat until a cube of bread browns in 30 seconds. Pat the chips dry with kitchen paper. Deep-fry in batches for 5 minutes until golden.

- Season the fish and dust with the cornflour. Dip into the batter until coated, shake off any excess and deep-fry in batches for 7 minutes, using tongs to turn the fish over. Drain on kitchen paper. Keep warm in a low oven. Increase the heat until a cube of bread browns in 15 seconds. Deep-fry the chips again in batches for 2 minutes until crisp and golden. Serve with the fish and mushy peas with lemon wedges on the side.

 Grilled Cod with Pea Salad

Brush 1 tablespoon olive oil over 4 x 175 g (6 oz) cod steaks. Cook on a smoking hot griddle pan for 3–5 minutes on each side. Meanwhile, whisk together 3 tablespoons olive oil and 1 tablespoon white wine vinegar. Season. Stir in some chopped chives. Boil 100 g (3½ oz) frozen peas for 3 minutes. Drain, cool under the cold tap and toss with the dressing. Slice 4 Little Gem lettuces into wedges. Serve with the peas, cod and crisps.

 Crispy Cod with Tartare Crust

Spread 1 tablespoon tartare sauce over each of 4 x 175 g (6 oz) skinless cod fillets. Place on a baking sheet and sprinkle over 75 g (3 oz) breadcrumbs. Place in a preheated oven, 200°C (400°F), Gas Mark 6, for 12–15 minutes until cooked through and crisp. Serve with some oven-baked chips.

20 Asian Seafood Noodles

Serves 4

100 g (3½ oz) pork fillet, cut into
thin strips

2 tablespoons sweet chilli sauce

2 tablespoons vegetable oil

1 red pepper, sliced

4 spring onions, sliced

2 garlic cloves, crushed

1 teaspoon finely chopped fresh
root ginger

1 tablespoon curry paste

100 g (3½ oz) raw squid rings

150 g (5 oz) cooked peeled small
prawns

300 g (10 oz) pack fresh egg
noodles

2 tablespoons soy sauce

50 g (2 oz) bean sprouts

- Toss the pork strips in the sweet chilli sauce. Cook under a preheated hot grill for 7 minutes, turning once, until cooked through, then keep warm.

- Heat a wok until smoking, then pour in the oil. Stir-fry the red pepper for 1 minute. Add the spring onions, garlic and ginger and toss around the pan, then stir in the curry paste followed by the squid rings. Stir-fry for 1 minute until the squid is cooked through.

- Add the prawns, noodles, soy sauce, bean sprouts and pork to the wok, with a splash of boiling water if necessary. Toss around the pan until heated through, then divide into serving bowls and serve immediately.

---

10 Spicy Prawn Noodles

Heat 1 tablespoon curry paste in a saucepan. Add 2 chopped spring onions and 2 grated carrots and cook for 2 minutes until softened. Add 1.2 litres (2 pints) vegetable stock, 300 g (10 oz) straight-to-wok noodles and 200 g (7 oz) cooked peeled large prawns. Heat through, then sprinkle with sesame seeds to serve.

30 Pork with Prawn Noodles

Rub 3 tablespoons hoisin sauce over 450 g (14½ oz) pork tenderloin. Place on a lightly oiled baking sheet. Drizzle with 1 tablespoon vegetable oil. Place in a preheated oven, 220°C (425°F), Gas Mark 7, for 20–25 minutes until cooked through. Meanwhile, heat 1 tablespoon vegetable oil in a wok. Add 4 sliced spring onions, 2 crushed garlic cloves and 1 teaspoon finely chopped fresh root ginger. Stir-fry for 1 minute. Add 150 g (5 oz) cooked peeled prawns and a 300 g (10 oz) pack fresh egg noodles. Heat through. Mix together 2 tablespoons soy sauce, 1 tablespoon sweet chilli sauce, a squeeze of lime juice and 1 teaspoon cornflour. Add to the wok with 3 tablespoons water. Cook, stirring, until thickened. Cut the pork into thick slices. Serve with the noodles.

 Trout and Bacon Hash

Serves 3–4

500 g (1 lb) new potatoes, halved
15 g (½ oz) butter
375 g (12 oz) trout fillets
4 streaky bacon rashers
3 tablespoons olive oil
1 onion, thinly sliced
salt and pepper
handful of flat leaf parsley,
 chopped, to garnish

- Cook the potatoes in a saucepan of lightly salted boiling water for about 10 minutes until just tender, then drain.

- Meanwhile, dot the butter over the trout, season and cook under a preheated hot grill for 7–10 minutes until cooked through. Remove from the grill and set aside, keeping the grill on. Cook the bacon under the grill until crispy. When the fish is cool enough to handle, discard the skin and break the flesh into large flakes.

- Heat 2 tablespoons of the oil in a large frying pan. Add the onion and cook for 5 minutes until softened. Add the remaining oil to the frying pan and add the potatoes. Cook until browned and crisp all over. Break the bacon into pieces, add to the pan with the trout and heat through. Serve scattered with the parsley.

 Bacon and Smoked Trout Gnocchi

Cook 4 streaky bacon rashers under a preheated hot grill until crispy. Meanwhile, cook 400 g (13 oz) potato gnocchi according to the pack instructions. Drain and mix with 150 g (5 oz) skinless smoked trout fillets, broken into chunks, 1 teaspoon wholegrain mustard and 2 tablespoons olive oil. Crumble over the bacon to serve.

 Trout and Bacon Hash with Poached Eggs Prepare the hash as above. While the trout and bacon are cooking, heat a small saucepan of water until simmering. Use a spoon and vigorously stir to make a whirlpool in the pan. Crack 1 egg into a small cup and gently slide into the centre of the whirlpool. Cook for 3–4 minutes until just cooked through. Remove from pan and pat dry with kitchen paper. Keep warm. Repeat with another 2 or 3 eggs, depending on whether you are serving 3 or 4 people. Top each serving of the hash with a poached egg.

Honey Mustard Salmon

Serves 4

4 salmon fillets, about 150 g
  (5 oz) each
olive oil, for oiling
2 tablespoons wholegrain mustard
2 tablespoons clear honey
handful of dill, chopped
salt and pepper

- Place the salmon on a lightly oiled baking tin and season. Mix together the mustard, honey and dill and drizzle over the salmon.

- Place in a preheated oven, 220°C (425°F), Gas Mark 7, for 8 minutes or until cooked through. Serve with some new potatoes and a cucumber salad.

 ### Mustard Salmon Burgers

In a food processor, whizz 500 g (1 lb) skinless salmon fillets to a rough paste. Mix with a handful of breadcrumbs and 1 beaten egg. Lightly wet your hands, then shape into 4 patties. Heat 1 tablespoon vegetable oil in a frying pan and cook for 5–7 minutes on each side until cooked through. Meanwhile, mix together 4 tablespoons mayonnaise, 1 tablespoon wholegrain mustard and 2 teaspoons chopped dill. Place each salmon burger in a split and toasted burger bun and top with some cucumber slices and a dollop of mayonnaise.

Salmon with Mustard

Hollandaise Place 4 x 125 g (4 oz) thin salmon fillets on a lightly oiled baking sheet, drizzle over 2 tablespoons olive oil and season. Place in a preheated oven, 120°C (250°F), Gas Mark ½, for 25–30 minutes until just cooked through. Meanwhile, crack 2 egg yolks into a heatproof bowl set snugly over a saucepan of simmering water. Add a squeeze of lemon juice and then slowly whisk in 100 g (3½ oz) melted butter until the sauce has thickened. Stir in 1 teaspoon wholegrain mustard and more lemon juice to taste. Serve with the salmon.

30 Salmon Fishcakes with Dill Sauce

Serves 4

450 g (14½ oz) potatoes, peeled
and cubed
3 tablespoons olive oil
500 g (1 lb) skinless salmon fillet
1 tablespoon chopped dill
finely grated rind of 1 lemon
plain flour, for dusting
1 egg, beaten
75 g (3 oz) dried breadcrumbs
salt and pepper
green salad, to serve

For the dill sauce

3 tablespoons mayonnaise
3 tablespoons natural yogurt
handful of dill, chopped
1 cornichon, sliced

- Cook the potatoes in a saucepan of lightly salted boiling water for 12 minutes until soft. Drain well and roughly mash.

- Meanwhile, rub 1 teaspoon of the oil over the salmon and season well. Cook under a preheated hot grill for 10 minutes until cooked through. Leave to cool a little, then break into large flakes. Mix together the ingredients for the sauce.

- Mix together the potato, salmon, dill and lemon rind. Lightly wet your hands, then shape into 8 fishcakes. Dust each fishcake with a little flour, dip into the egg and finally dip into the breadcrumbs until well coated.

- Heat the remaining oil in a large, nonstick frying pan. Cook the fishcakes for 3–4 minutes on each side until golden and crisp. Serve with a green salad and the dill sauce.

 Easy Salmon and Potato Salad

Discard the skin and any bones from 1 x 150 g (5 oz) hot-smoked salmon fillet, then flake. Stir into a 500 g (1 lb) tub shop-bought creamy plain potato salad along with a handful of chopped dill and 1 sliced cornichon. Serve with strips of pitta bread toasted until crisp.

 Moroccan-Style Salmon Cakes

Place 200 g (7 oz) couscous in a heatproof bowl. Pour over 250 ml (8 fl oz) boiling water and season with salt. Cover with clingfilm and leave to stand for about 7 minutes until swelled. Uncover and leave to cool a little, then mix with a drained 400 g (13 oz) can salmon or tuna, 1 beaten egg, a handful of coriander, chopped, and 1–2 teaspoons harissa spice mix. Lightly wet your hands, then form into 4 fishcakes. Heat 1 tablespoon olive oil in a large, nonstick frying pan. Add the fishcakes and cook for 3–5 minutes on each side until browned, then serve.

30 Spicy Tuna Empanadas

Serves 4

375 g (12 oz) ready-rolled puff
pastry

200 g (7 oz) can tuna in spring
water, drained

100 ml (3½ fl oz) shop-bought
tomato pasta sauce

1 teaspoon smoked paprika

1 ready-roasted red pepper,
chopped

1 egg yolk, beaten

salt and pepper

- Use a small dinner plate, about 15 cm (6 inches) in diameter, to cut out 4 rounds from the pastry. Mix together the tuna, tomato sauce, paprika and red pepper. Spoon about 2 tablespoons of the mixture on to one side of each circle.

- Brush around the edge of each pastry round with a little of the egg. Fold over the pastry, squeeze out any air and use your hands or a fork to seal the edges. Place on a baking sheet and brush all over with more of the egg.

- Place in a preheated oven, 200°C (400°F), Gas Mark 6, for 15 minutes, or until crisp.

10 Spicy Tuna Melts

Mix together a drained 200 g (7 oz) can tuna in spring water, 4 tablespoons mayonnaise and 1 teaspoon smoked paprika. Lightly toast 4 slices of bread. Spread all over with the tuna mixture, then place a layer of sliced Cheddar cheese on top. Cover with some sliced tomato and then more cheese slices. Cook under a preheated hot grill for 3–5 minutes until melted and bubbling.

20 Tuna Steak Salad with Pitta Crisps

Cut 5 plum tomatoes into wedges and thinly slice ½ red onion. Whisk together 1 tablespoon sherry vinegar and 3 tablespoons olive oil. Toss with the tomato and onion and ½ finely chopped red chilli. Brush olive oil over 4 x 150 g (5 oz) tuna steaks and cook on a smoking hot griddle pan for 3–5 minutes on each side until cooked through. Meanwhile, brush olive oil over

1 pitta bread, split in half and then cut into pieces. Cook under a preheated hot grill until crisp. Toss the tomato and onion salad with the leaves of 1 Cos lettuce. Arrange on a serving plate with the tuna steaks and serve with the pitta crisps alongside.

20 Salmon Tikka Masala

Serves 4

2 tablespoons vegetable oil

1 onion, sliced

1 garlic clove, crushed

1 teaspoon grated fresh root
ginger

1 red pepper, sliced

3 tablespoons tikka masala paste

400 g (13 oz) can chopped
tomatoes

375 g (12 oz) salmon fillet, cut into
chunks

75 ml (3 fl oz) single cream

75 ml (3 fl oz) natural yogurt

salt and pepper

handful of coriander, chopped,
to garnish

naan bread, to serve

• Heat the oil in a large saucepan. Add the onion, garlic and ginger and cook for 3 minutes until softened. Add the red pepper and cook for a further 2 minutes. Stir in the tikka masala paste followed by the tomatoes and bring to the boil. Cook for 5 minutes.

• Reduce to a simmer, add the salmon and season. Cook for 8 minutes or until cooked through. Stir through the cream and some of the yogurt leaving a little to drizzle on top, then scatter with the coriander before serving with naan bread.

---

10 Salmon Tikka Wraps

Mix 3 tablespoons tikka masala paste with 3 tablespoons natural yogurt. Spread over 4 x 100 g (3½ oz) thin salmon fillets. Cook under a preheated hot grill for 7 minutes until cooked through. Break the fish into flakes, discarding the skin and any bones. Divide between 4 chapatis with some chopped lettuce, cucumber and more yogurt. Roll up to serve.

30 Salmon with Homemade Masala

Paste Mix together 2 tablespoons tomato purée, 1 tablespoon ground cumin, 2 teaspoons ground coriander, 1 teaspoon smoked paprika and a pinch of caster sugar. Heat 2 tablespoons vegetable oil in a saucepan. Add 1 finely chopped onion, 1 crushed garlic clove and 1 teaspoon grated fresh root ginger. Cook for 3 minutes until softened. Stir in half the spice paste followed by a 400 g (13 oz) can chopped tomatoes. Bring to the boil, then simmer for 20 minutes. Meanwhile, mix the remaining paste with 3 tablespoons vegetable oil. Spread over 4 x 100 g (3½ oz) thin salmon fillets. Cook under a preheated medium grill for 10 minutes until charred and cooked through. Spoon the curry sauce over the salmon. Drizzle with natural yogurt before serving.

30 Crunchy Sardine Caesar Salad

Serves 4

2 eggs
1 garlic clove, crushed
juice of ½ lemon
½ teaspoon Worcestershire sauce
125 ml (4 fl oz) extra virgin
  olive oil
50 g (2 oz) breadcrumbs
25 g (1 oz) Parmesan cheese,
  grated, plus extra to serve
2 tablespoons milk
8 sardines, filleted and halved
vegetable oil, for deep-frying
1 large Cos lettuce, sliced
salt and pepper

• Crack 1 egg into a saucepan of boiling water and cook for just 45 seconds. Leave to cool a little, then whizz in a food processor with the garlic, lemon juice and Worcestershire sauce. With the motor running, slowly add the oil in a thin stream until thickened. Season and set aside.

• Mix together the breadcrumbs and Parmesan and place in a large freezer bag. Beat together the remaining egg and the milk. Dip the sardines into the egg mixture until coated, shake off any excess, then place in the freezer bag and shake until coated.

• Fill a large, deep saucepan one-third full with oil and heat until a cube of bread browns in 15 seconds. Deep-fry the sardines in batches for 3–5 minutes until golden and crisp. Drain on kitchen paper.

• Place the lettuce on serving plates. Arrange the sardines on top, then drizzle over the dressing and shave some Parmesan on top.

---

1 Easy Caesar Salad

Stir 1 crushed garlic clove and 25 g (1 oz) grated Parmesan cheese into 5 tablespoons mayonnaise. Tear ¼ baguette into chunks. Toast under a preheated hot grill. Toss 1 sliced Cos lettuce with the mayonnaise, toasted chunks of baguette and a handful of marinated sardines or herrings.

2 Crunchy Fishcake Salad

Drain 2 x 200 g (7 oz) cans tuna and 1 x 125 g (4 oz) can smoked tuna. Beat together 2 eggs, then use a little of the egg to mix together the tuna and 1 finely chopped spring onion. Lightly wet your hands, then shape into 4 fishcakes. Dust with plain flour, then dip into the remaining egg. Press 50 g (2 oz) breadcrumbs all over. Heat 3 tablespoons olive oil in a large, nonstick frying pan. Cook the fishcakes for 3–4 minutes on each side until golden and crisp. Meanwhile, stir 1 small crushed garlic clove into 6 tablespoons mayonnaise along with a squeeze of lemon juice and 15 g (½ oz) grated Parmesan cheese. Arrange a fishcake and a handful of green salad leaves on each of 4 serving plates. Spoon over the mayonnaise to serve.

Mini Seafood Pizza Bites

Serves 4

4 mini pitta breads
2 tablespoons olive oil
1 garlic clove, peeled and halved
100 ml (3½ fl oz) shop-bought
   tomato and basil sauce
1 tablespoon tomato purée
125 g (4 oz) cooked peeled
   prawns, halved
1 ready-roasted red pepper, torn
   into strips
125 g (4 oz) mozzarella cheese,
   torn into strips
salt and pepper
handful of basil, torn into small
   pieces, to garnish

- Split the pitta breads into 2 thin halves and drizzle the oil over the inside sides. Toast, inside-side up, under a preheated hot grill for 2–3 minutes until crisp. Rub all over with the garlic clove halves.

- Meanwhile, mix together the tomato sauce and tomato purée and season. Spoon over the toasted sides of the bread. Arrange the prawns, red pepper and mozzarella on top. Place back under the grill and cook for 3–5 minutes until the cheese has melted. Scatter over the basil and serve.

 Speedy Seafood Pizza

Mix together 100 ml (3½ fl oz) shop-bought tomato and basil sauce and 3 tablespoons tomato purée. Spread over a shop-bought pizza base set on a baking sheet. Heat 1 tablespoon olive oil in a frying pan. Cook 125 g (4 oz) raw peeled prawns, 50 g (2 oz) raw squid rings and 1 crushed garlic clove for 3–5 minutes until cooked through. Scatter over the pizza with 1 ready-roasted red pepper and 125 g (4 oz) mozzarella cheese, both torn into strips. Place in a preheated oven, 200°C (400°F), Gas Mark 6, for 10 minutes, then serve.

 Homemade Seafood Pizzas

Mix together 250 g (8 oz) strong white bread flour, 1 teaspoon dried yeast and ½ teaspoon salt. Pour over 150 ml (¼ pint) warm water and 1 tablespoon olive oil. Stir until the mixture comes together into a dough. Knead a couple of times on a floured surface. Divide into 4 and roll out as thinly as you can. Place on baking sheets. Mix together 100 ml (3½ fl oz) shop-bought tomato and basil sauce and 3 tablespoons tomato purée. Spread over the pizza bases. Top with 125 g (4 oz) raw peeled prawns, 200 g (7 oz) cleaned live clams and 125 g (4 oz) sliced mozzarella cheese, divided between the pizza bases, then sprinkle with chilli flakes and dried oregano. Place in a preheated oven, 240°C (475°F), Gas Mark 9, for 10–15 minutes until cooked through. Discard any clams that remain closed.

Pan-Fried Red Mullet with Herby Potato Salad

Serves 4

750 g (1½ lb) new potatoes, halved
5 tablespoons extra virgin olive oil
finely grated rind and juice of 1 lemon
4 red mullet fillets, about 150 g (5 oz) each
4 spring onions, sliced
½ red chilli, finely chopped
handful of basil and parsley leaves, chopped
salt and pepper

• Cook the potatoes in a saucepan of lightly salted boiling water for 12 minutes until tender, then drain and thickly slice. Toss with 4 tablespoons of the oil and the lemon rind and juice, season with salt and pepper and leave to cool a little.

• Meanwhile, heat the remaining oil in a large frying pan. Add the fish fillets skin-side down, season and cook for 5 minutes. Turn over and cook for a further 3–5 minutes or until cooked through.

• Stir the spring onions, chilli and herbs through the potatoes and serve with the fish.

Herby Fish Strips with Couscous

Place 400 g (13 oz) couscous in a heatproof bowl. Pour over 500 ml (17 fl oz) boiling water, add a knob of butter and season with salt. Cover with clingfilm and leave for 7–10 minutes until swelled. Meanwhile, cut 4 x 200 g (7 oz) red mullet fillets into thin strips and season. Mix together 2 tablespoons olive oil, ½ finely chopped red chilli and a handful of basil and flat leaf parsley, chopped. Toss with the fish. Cook under a preheated hot grill for 3–5 minutes on each side until cooked through. Serve with the couscous and a green salad.

Spiced Fish with Herby Pilaff

Heat 25 g (1 oz) butter in a saucepan. Add 1 each finely chopped onion and garlic clove and cook for a few minutes until softened. Add 200 g (7 oz) basmati rice, stir around to coat, then pour over 750 ml (1¼ pints) hot vegetable stock. Bring to the boil and cook for about 10 minutes until the liquid has nearly boiled away and small craters appear in the rice. Cover with a tight-fitting lid and leave to stand for 10 minutes. Meanwhile, rub 1 tablespoon olive oil over 4 x 200 g (7 oz) red mullet fillets, then sprinkle with ½ teaspoon each ground cumin and paprika. Cook under a preheated hot grill for 7–10 minutes until cooked through. Stir a handful of basil and flat leaf parsley, chopped, through the rice along with the finely grated rind of ½ lemon and a squeeze of lemon juice. Serve alongside the fish.

Crispy Salmon and Pesto Parcels

Serves 4

50 g (2 oz) butter, melted
4 tablespoons olive oil
4 large sheets of filo pastry
4 skinless salmon fillets, about
   150 g (5 oz) each
4 tablespoons fresh green pesto
4 tablespoons cream cheese
salt and pepper
tomato salad, to serve

- Stir together the melted butter and oil. Use a pastry brush to brush the mixture all over 1 sheet of filo pastry (cover the remaining pastry with a damp but not wet piece of kitchen paper).

- Place 1 salmon fillet at one end of the sheet and season. Mix together the pesto and cream cheese and spread a little over the top of the salmon. Fold over the ends of the pastry, then roll up so that the salmon is enclosed. Place it, seam-side down (you may have to trim the edge), on a baking sheet and brush all over with more of the butter mixture. Repeat with the remaining salmon fillets.

- Place in a preheated oven, 220°C (425°F), Gas Mark 7, for 15 minutes until browned and crisp. Serve with a tomato salad.

 Smoked Salmon, Cheese and Pesto Rotolos Spread 3 tablespoons cream cheese all over each of 2 wraps. Scatter 1 slice of smoked salmon, cut into strips, and drizzle 2 teaspoons fresh green pesto over each wrap. Tightly roll up the wraps, then use a sharp knife to trim the ends and slice into bite-sized pieces. Serve with a mixed leaf salad.

 Salmon, Pea and Pesto Soup Melt 15 g (½ oz) butter in a saucepan. Add 1 finely chopped onion and 1 crushed garlic clove and cook for about 5 minutes until softened. Pour over 750 ml (1¼ pints) chicken stock and bring to the boil. Leave to simmer for 2 minutes, then add 1 finely chopped courgette and cook for a further 1–2 minutes.

Stir through 100 g (3½ oz) frozen peas and 4 tablespoons fresh green pesto and cook for a further 3 minutes. Remove the skin from a 175 g (6 oz) hot-smoked salmon fillet and break into chunks. Add to the soup and heat through. Swirl over 2 tablespoons crème fraîche before serving.

20 Sweet and Sour Fish

Serves 4

vegetable oil, for frying

1 onion, sliced

1 tablespoon thinly sliced fresh
  root ginger

3 garlic cloves, crushed

1 red pepper, sliced

2 tablespoons tomato ketchup

2 tablespoons rice vinegar

2 tablespoons caster sugar

1 tablespoon soy sauce

1 teaspoon cornflour

100 g (3½ oz) self-raising flour

1 egg, beaten

400 g (13 oz) sea bass fillet,
  skinned, if you like, and cut into
  chunks

2 spring onions, sliced

salt and pepper

- Heat 1 tablespoon oil in a wok. Add the onion and stir-fry for 2 minutes. Add the ginger, garlic and red pepper and stir-fry for 2 minutes until softened. Mix together the ketchup, vinegar, sugar, soy sauce, 150 ml (¼ pint) water and the cornflour until smooth. Stir into the wok and cook for 3–5 minutes until thickened. Keep warm.

- Fill a large, deep saucepan one-third full with oil and heat until a cube of bread browns in 15 seconds. Beat together the flour, egg and 125 ml (4 fl oz) iced water (don't worry if there are still a few lumps), then season well. Dip the fish into the batter until coated, shake off any excess and deep-fry in 2 batches for 3–4 minutes until golden brown all over. Drain on kitchen paper.

- Stir the fish into the sauce, then serve immediately with the spring onions scattered over.

---

10 Sweet and Sour Prawn Noodles

Stir-fry a 300 g (10 oz) pack stir-fry vegetables in a wok in a little vegetable oil. Add 100 g (3½ oz) cooked peeled prawns and 300 g (10 oz) fresh egg noodles. In a small bowl, mix 2 tablespoons each tomato ketchup, rice vinegar and caster sugar, 1 tablespoon soy sauce, 150 ml (¼ pint) water and 1 teaspoon cornflour. Add to the wok and cook, stirring, for 3–5 minutes until thickened. Serve.

30 Marinated Sweet and Sour Fish

Marinate 400 g (13 oz) sea bass fillet, skinned and cut into chunks, in 1 tablespoon each soy sauce and sherry for 15 minutes. Meanwhile, stir-fry 1 sliced onion, 3 crushed garlic cloves and 1 tablespoon thinly sliced fresh root ginger in 1 tablespoon vegetable oil for 5 minutes until softened. Stir in 3 tablespoons each soy sauce, sherry and water and 1 teaspoon clear honey. Simmer until sticky and keep warm. Fill a large, deep saucepan one-third full with oil and heat until a cube of bread browns in 15 seconds. Beat together 100 g (3½ oz) self-raising flour, 1 beaten egg and 125 ml (4 fl oz) iced water. Season well. Pat the fish dry. Dip in the batter until coated. Deep-fry in 2 batches for 3–4 minutes until golden brown. Drizzle over the sauce.

Crispy Lemon Prawn Skewers

Serves 4

300 g (10 oz) cooked peeled
   large prawns
3 tablespoons olive oil
100 g (3½ oz) dried breadcrumbs
1 garlic clove, crushed
finely grated rind of 1 lemon
handful of oregano leaves,
   finely chopped
salt and pepper
lemon wedges, to serve

- Pat the prawns dry with kitchen paper, then season and rub all over with the oil. Thread on to metal skewers.

- Mix together the remaining ingredients and place on a plate. Roll the skewered prawns in the breadcrumb mixture to coat all over. Cook under a hot grill for 2 minutes. Turn over and cook for a further 1–2 minutes until golden, then serve with lemon wedges.

Sticky Lemon Prawn Noodles

Cook 300 g (10 oz) dried medium egg noodles according to the pack instructions, then drain. Meanwhile, heat 2 tablespoons vegetable oil in a wok or large frying pan over a high heat. Add 2 sliced spring onions, 2 chopped garlic cloves, 1 teaspoon finely chopped fresh root ginger, 1 sliced red onion and 100 g (3½ oz) mangetout. Stir-fry for 5 minutes. Add 250 g (8 oz) raw peeled large prawns. Stir-fry for 5 minutes until cooked through. Mix 1 teaspoon cornflour with 2 tablespoons soy sauce, the juice of 1 lemon, 1 tablespoon clear honey and 4 tablespoons water, add and heat through. Add the noodles and cook for 2 minutes.

Fennel, Lemon and Prawn Risotto

Heat 1 tablespoon olive oil in a deep frying pan. Add 1 finely chopped onion, 1 chopped fennel bulb and 1 finely chopped garlic clove and cook for 5–7 minutes until softened. Stir in 300 g (10 oz) risotto rice until well coated. Pour in 150 ml (¼ pint) dry white wine and boil until reduced. Add about 1.5 litres (2½ pints) hot fish stock, a ladleful at a time, stirring and simmering after each addition until the stock is absorbed before adding the next. Continue until all the stock is absorbed, about 15 minutes. Add 250 g (8 oz) raw peeled large prawns and cook for a further 5 minutes until the rice is tender and the prawns are cooked through. Squeeze over the juice of 1 lemon and stir in 25 g (1 oz) grated Parmesan cheese and 15 g (½ oz) butter just before serving.

Cod with Lemon, Basil and Sun-Dried Tomato Crust

Serves 4

4 thick cod fillets, about 150 g (5 oz) each

2 tablespoons olive oil, plus extra for oiling

75 g (3 oz) breadcrumbs

4 sun-dried tomatoes, finely chopped

finely grated rind of 1 lemon

handful of basil, chopped

salt and pepper

- Season the cod, then place on a lightly oiled baking sheet. Rub 1 tablespoon of the oil over the top of the fish.

- Mix together all the remaining ingredients. Press on top of each fish fillet, then drizzle over the remaining oil. Place in a preheated oven, 200°C (400°F), Gas Mark 6, for 12–15 minutes until the fish is lightly crisp and cooked through. Serve with potatoes and a tomato salad.

 Tomato Pesto Cod Bites

Cut 4 x 150 g (5 oz) thick cod fillets into small pieces. Mix together 1 tablespoon olive oil and 2 tablespoons sun-dried tomato pesto, then toss with the fish. Place 75 g (3 oz) breadcrumbs and a handful of basil, chopped, in a large freezer bag, add the cod pieces and shake well until coated. Heat 2 tablespoons olive oil in a frying pan and cook the cod for 5 minutes, turning often, until cooked through, then serve.

 Cod with Lemon Pesto and Tomatoes

In a food processor, whizz together a large handful of basil, 25 g (1 oz) grated Parmesan cheese, 5 tablespoons extra virgin olive oil and the finely grated rind of ½ lemon until you have a paste. Heat a small dry pan and cook 25 g (1 oz) pine nuts until lightly browned all over. Leave to cool a little. Roughly chop and add to the paste. Place 4 x 150 g (5 oz) thick cod fillets on a baking sheet. Spread all over with the paste. Thinly slice 2 tomatoes and arrange on top. Place in a preheated oven, 200°C (400°F), Gas Mark 6, for 12–15 minutes until the fish is cooked through.

Serves 4

400 g (13 oz) potatoes, peeled
   and thickly sliced
150 g (5 oz) skinless salmon fillet
6 eggs, beaten
handful of dill, chopped
100 g (3½ oz) frozen peas
1 spring onion, sliced
1 tablespoon vegetable oil
salt and pepper
mixed salad leaves, to serve

- Cook the potatoes in a saucepan of lightly salted boiling water for 10 minutes until tender, then carefully drain.

- Meanwhile, place the salmon in a small saucepan. Cover with boiling water and leave to simmer for 7 minutes until the fish flakes easily. Drain, then break into large flakes.

- Mix together the eggs, dill, peas and spring onion, then season. Heat the oil in a 20 cm (8 inch) nonstick frying pan. Stir the potatoes and salmon into the egg mixture, then tip into the pan. Cook over a very low heat for 10–15 minutes until just set. Cut into wedges and serve with a mixed leaf salad.

 Pea and Salmon Omelettes

Cook 25 g (1 oz) frozen peas in boiling water for 3 minutes until cooked through, then drain. Beat 4 eggs together with some dill. Heat 15 g (½ oz) butter in small frying pan. Add a quarter of the egg mixture and swirl around the pan. Cook for 1 minute until the mixture is starting to set, then sprinkle over 1 teaspoon grated Parmesan cheese, a few of the peas and a slice of smoked salmon, cut into strips. Fold over the omelette and serve. Repeat with the remaining egg mixture.

 Pea and Smoked Salmon Soup

Heat 15 g (½ oz) butter in a saucepan. Add 1 finely chopped onion and cook for 5 minutes until softened. Pour over 750 ml (1¼ pints) hot chicken stock. Bring to the boil, then simmer and tip in 200 g (7 oz) frozen peas and a mint sprig. Cook for 3 minutes until the peas are tender. Use a stick blender to whizz until smooth. Stir in 2 tablespoons crème fraîche. Cut 75 g (3 oz) smoked salmon into thin strips and scatter over to serve.

20 Plaice Florentine

Serves 4

15 g (½ oz) butter, plus extra for greasing

1 tablespoon plain flour

150 ml (¼ pint) milk

50 g (2 oz) Cheddar cheese, grated

150 g (5 oz) frozen spinach

2 large plaice fillets, about 175 g (6 oz) each, halved to make 4 thin fillets

25 g (1 oz) Parmesan cheese, grated

salt and pepper

mashed potato, to serve

- Melt the butter in a saucepan. Stir in the flour and cook for 2 minutes. Slowly whisk in the milk until smooth. Bring to the boil, whisking, then simmer for a few minutes until thickened. Take off the heat, stir in the cheese and season.

- Place the spinach in a sieve and pour over boiling water until thawed. Drain well, then roughly chop. Place the fish on a lightly greased baking sheet. Spread a layer of spinach on top of each fillet, then drizzle over some of the white sauce. Sprinkle with the Parmesan.

- Place in a preheated oven, 200°C (400°F), Gas Mark 6, for 10–12 minutes until the fish is just cooked through. Serve immediately with mashed potato.

---

10 Plaice with Simple Parsley Sauce

Smear a little butter over 4 x 175 g (6 oz) plaice fillets. Cook under a preheated hot grill for 7–10 minutes until just cooked through. Meanwhile, mix 4 tablespoons crème fraîche with a large handful of parsley, chopped, and a little milk to loosen. Spoon over the fish and serve alongside some lightly cooked spinach and mashed canned butter beans warmed through in a saucepan.

30 Creamy Spinach and Plaice Pie

Place 300 g (10 oz) frozen spinach in a sieve and pour over boiling water until thawed. Arrange in the bottom of a baking dish. Poach 2 large plaice fillets, about 175 g (6 oz) each in a wide pan in 100 ml (3½ fl oz) dry white wine plus enough water to cover for 7–10 minutes until cooked through. Remove the fish. Boil the liquid until you have 100 ml (3½ fl oz) remaining. Melt 25 g (1 oz) butter in a saucepan. Stir in 25 g (1 oz) plain flour and cook for 2 minutes. Whisk in the reduced poaching liquid followed by 200 ml (7 fl oz) milk until smooth. Bring to the boil, whisking, then simmer for a few minutes until thickened. Take off the heat and stir in 2 tablespoons crème fraîche, 25 g (1 oz) grated Parmesan cheese and 1 egg yolk. Place the cooked fish on top of the spinach, pour over the sauce and cook under a hot grill for 3–5 minutes until browned.

10 Simple Tuna Pasta

Serves 4

400 g (13 oz) quick-cook penne
50 g (2 oz) anchovy fillets in oil
2 garlic cloves, crushed
1 chilli, deseeded and chopped
  (optional)
200 g (7 oz) can tuna in spring
  water, drained
lemon juice, to taste
handful of flat leaf parsley,
  chopped
pepper

- Cook the pasta according to the pack instructions.

- Meanwhile, drain the anchovies, reserving the oil. Heat a little of the reserved oil in a small frying pan. Add the anchovies, garlic and chilli, if using, and cook for about 3 minutes until the anchovies have dissolved into the oil. Stir in the tuna and lemon juice to taste, then season with plenty of pepper.

- Drain the pasta, reserving a little of the cooking water. Return to the pan and stir through the tuna sauce and most of the parsley. Add some of the reserved cooking water to loosen the mixture if necessary. Scatter with the remaining parsley to serve.

2 Tuna Ball Pasta

Tip a drained 200 g (7 oz) can tuna in spring water into a bowl. Add 1 beaten egg and a pinch of chilli flakes. Stir together. Lightly wet your hands, then shape into small balls. Heat 1 tablespoon olive oil in a frying pan. Cook the tuna balls for 10 minutes until golden all over. Heat 325 g (11 oz) shop-bought tomato and basil pasta sauce in a saucepan. Add the tuna balls and cook for 5 minutes. Meanwhile, cook 400 g (13 oz) quick-cook penne according to the pack instructions. Drain and stir through the sauce. Top with some chopped basil before serving.

3 Tuna and Sweetcorn Pasta

Bake Cook 400 g (13 oz) dried penne according to the pack instructions. Meanwhile, melt 40 g (1½ oz) butter in a saucepan, stir in 40 g (1½ oz) plain flour and cook for 2 minutes. Slowly whisk in 575 ml (18 fl oz) milk until smooth. Bring to the boil, whisking, then simmer until thickened. Drain the pasta. Mix with the sauce and a 200 g (7 oz) can tuna in spring water and a drained 200 g (7 oz) can sweetcorn kernels. Pour into a baking dish, scatter over 75 g (3 oz) dried breadcrumbs and place in a preheated oven, 200 °C (400 °F), Gas Mark 6, for 15 minutes until golden and bubbling.

Fish Tortillas with Avocado Salsa

Serves 4

1 avocado
handful of coriander, chopped,
   plus extra to serve
1 tablespoon vegetable oil
1 teaspoon ground cumin
1 teaspoon paprika
handful of thyme, chopped
6 skinless gurnard fillets,
   about 100 g (3½ oz) each,
   cut into strips
8 soft flour tortillas
100 g (3½ oz) radishes, thinly
   sliced
1 lime, cut into wedges
50 ml (2 fl oz) soured cream
salt and pepper

- Cut the avocado in half and discard the stone. Peel, then cut into slices.

- Heat a griddle pan. Mix together the coriander, the oil, cumin, paprika and thyme, then season. Rub over the fish strips, then cook on the griddle pan for 2 minutes on each side until cooked through.

- Meanwhile, warm the tortillas in a microwave or in the oven according to the pack instructions.

- Set out the avocado, radishes, lime wedges and soured cream on a serving board. Place a little of the fish, avocado, vegetables and a squeeze of lime in each tortilla and top with soured cream and some coriander sprigs, roll up and eat.

Spicy Tuna Tortilla Wraps

Mix together a drained 200 g (7 oz) can tuna, 1 chopped tomato, 1 chopped red pepper, 5 tablespoons mayonnaise and 2 drops of Tabasco sauce. Spread over 4 soft flour tortillas, roll up and serve.

Fish Tortillas with Pepper Salsa

Rub a little olive oil over 2 red peppers and 1 red chilli. Cook under a hot grill for 10–15 minutes until blackened all over. Seal in a freezer bag for 5 minutes. Meanwhile, mix together 25 g (1 oz) chopped coriander, 1 tablespoon vegetable oil, 1 teaspoon each ground cumin and paprika and a handful of thyme, chopped. Season with salt and pepper. Rub over 4 x 100 g (3½ oz) skinless gurnard fillets. Cook on a hot griddle pan for 2 minutes on each side. Warm 6 soft flour tortillas according to the pack instructions. Peel away the skin of the pepper, discard the core and seeds and finely chop. Mix with 1 finely chopped shallot, 2 tablespoons olive oil and 2 teaspoons sherry vinegar. Wrap the fish and salsa in the tortillas.

3 Fish Pie

Serves 4

750 g (1½ lb) potatoes, peeled and cut into small chunks
200 g (7 oz) crème fraîche
25 g (1 oz) butter, plus extra for greasing
1 tablespoon olive oil
400 g (13 oz) baby spinach leaves
4 eggs
400 g (13 oz) skinless coley fillet, cut into large chunks
handful of flat leaf parsley, chopped
salt and pepper

- Cook the potatoes in a saucepan of lightly salted boiling water for 8–10 minutes until soft. Drain and mash with 4 tablespoons of the crème fraîche and the butter, then season with salt and pepper.

- Meanwhile, heat the oil in a frying pan, add the spinach and a splash of water and cook until wilted. Drain really well.

- Arrange the spinach in the bottom of a greased baking dish, leaving 4 gaps for the eggs. Crack an egg into each gap. Scatter over the fish. Mix together the remaining crème fraîche with 5 tablespoons water and the parsley, season and then spoon over. Spread the mash on top.

- Place in a preheated oven, 220°C (425°F), Gas Mark 7, for about 15 minutes until golden and bubbling.

---

1 Fish Pie Fillets

Mix together 100 g (3½ oz) cream cheese and a handful of flat leaf parsley, chopped. Place 100 g (3½ oz) frozen spinach in a sieve. Pour over boiling water until wilted, then drain well and finely chop. Spread over 4 x 125 g (4 oz) thin white fish fillets. Top with the cream cheese and scatter over 50 g (2 oz) dried breadcrumbs. Cook under a preheated hot grill for 7 minutes, or until the fish is cooked through, then serve.

2 Quick Crispy Fish Pie

Melt 25 g (1 oz) butter and mix with 3 tablespoons olive oil. Brush over 1 sheet of filo pastry, place another sheet of filo on top and brush again, then repeat once more so that you have 3 layers. Loosely scrunch up the pastry so that it will fit on top of a baking dish. Transfer to a baking sheet and place in a preheated oven, 220°C (425°F), Gas Mark 7, for 10–15 minutes until crisp. Meanwhile, mix together 150 g (5 oz) crème fraîche, 5 tablespoons water and a handful of flat leaf parsley, chopped. Place 400 g (13 oz) skinless haddock fillet, cut into large chunks, into a saucepan, cover with the crème fraîche mixture and simmer for 7–10 minutes until cooked through. Place 200 g (7 oz) frozen spinach in a sieve. Pour over boiling water until wilted, then drain and arrange in the bottom of a baking dish. Spoon over the fish mixture and top with the baked filo.

30 Salmon and Leek Cannelloni

Serves 4

500 ml (17 fl oz) hot vegetable or
fish stock

3 leeks, thinly sliced

2 salmon fillets, about 150 g (5 oz)
each, cut into chunks

200 g (7 oz) crème fraîche

8 fresh lasagne sheets

50 g (2 oz) dried breadcrumbs

salt and pepper

- Pour half the hot stock over the leeks in a saucepan and boil for 5 minutes until soft. Pour the remaining stock over the salmon in a separate saucepan and simmer for 5 minutes until the fish flakes easily. Drain both, reserving the stock. Mix the stock with the crème fraîche. Flake the fish, discarding the skin and any bones.

- Stir together the leeks and salmon with 6 tablespoons of the crème fraîche mixture to loosen, then season. Place some of the mixture along one long side of a lasagne sheet. Roll up and place, seam-side down, in a baking dish. Repeat with the remaining lasagne sheets. Pour over the remaining crème fraîche mixture and sprinkle with the breadcrumbs.

- Place in a preheated oven, 200°C (400°F), Gas Mark 6, for 15–20 minutes until golden and cooked through.

10 Leek and Salmon Linguine

Cook 400 g (13 oz) dried linguine according to the packet instructions, adding 3 thinly sliced leeks for the last 5 minutes of cooking. Drain and then stir through 100 g (3½ oz) chopped smoked salmon and 5 tablespoons crème fraîche.

20 Salmon with a Creamy Leek

Topping Heat 25 g (1 oz) butter with a little water in a saucepan, add 3 thinly sliced leeks and cook for 10 minutes until soft. Stir in 100 g (3½ oz) crème fraîche and 1 teaspoon wholegrain mustard. Place 4 x 150 g (5 oz) salmon fillets on a baking sheet, skin-side down. Spread the leek mixture on top and cook under a preheated hot grill for 7–10 minutes until cooked through.

30 New Orleans Jambalaya

Serves 4

2 tablespoons vegetable oil
175 g (6 oz) andouille, kabanos or
  other smoked sausage, sliced
1 onion, finely chopped
2 celery sticks, chopped
1 green pepper, chopped
2 garlic cloves, finely chopped
½ teaspoon cayenne
200 g (7 oz) white long-grain rice
200 g (7 oz) can chopped
  tomatoes
500 ml (17 fl oz) fish or chicken
  stock
1 bay leaf
leaves from 1 thyme sprig,
  chopped
300 g (10 oz) raw peeled large
  prawns
Tabasco sauce, to taste
salt and pepper

- Heat the oil in a large, heavy-based saucepan. Add the sausage and cook for 3 minutes until browned. Add the onion, celery, green pepper and garlic and cook until softened. Add the cayenne followed by the rice and stir around the pan until well coated.

- Add the tomatoes to the pan, followed by the stock and herbs, then season. Bring to the boil, then cover and simmer for 15 minutes. Stir in the prawns, add a few drops of Tabasco sauce and leave to cook for a further 3–5 minutes until cooked through.

---

10 New Orleans Skewers

Thread 150 g (5 oz) cooked chunks of chorizo, 150 g (5 oz) cooked large prawns, 1 thickly sliced green pepper and a handful of cherry tomatoes on to metal skewers. Rub with olive oil and sprinkle with cayenne. Cook under a preheated hot grill for 2–3 minutes on each side, then serve.

20 New Orleans-Style Spaghetti

Heat 1 tablespoon olive oil in a saucepan. Cook 125 g (4 oz) sliced chorizo for 3 minutes. Remove. Add 1 finely chopped onion and 2 crushed garlic cloves and cook for 3 minutes. Add 1 tablespoon tomato purée, a pinch of sugar, a 400 g (13 oz) can chopped tomatoes and 200 ml (7 fl oz) water. Bring to the boil, then simmer for 8 minutes. Whizz until smooth with a stick blender. Return the chorizo to the pan with 1 ready-roasted pepper, cut into pieces, and 150 g (5 oz) cooked peeled large prawns. Heat through. Meanwhile, cook 400 g (13 oz) dried spaghetti according to the pack instructions. Drain, then toss with the sauce.

FIS-FAMI-NUK

Smoked Haddock Rarebit

Serves 4

300 g (10 oz) smoked
   haddock fillet
200 ml (7 fl oz) milk
15 g (½ oz) butter
1 tablespoon plain flour
2 tablespoons ale (optional)
75 g (3 oz) Cheddar cheese,
   grated
½ teaspoon wholegrain mustard
8 large slices of country-style
   bread, lightly toasted
salt and pepper
watercress salad, to serve

- Place the haddock in a shallow saucepan. Pour over the milk and simmer for 5–7 minutes until the fish flakes easily. Strain off the milk through a sieve and reserve. Break the fish into large flakes, discarding the skin and any bones.

- Melt the butter in a separate saucepan. Stir in the flour and cook for 2 minutes. Slowly start to whisk in the ale, if using, followed by the reserved poaching milk until smooth. Bring to the boil, whisking, then simmer for a few minutes until thickened. Take off the heat and stir in the cheese, mustard and haddock.

- Spread the mixture over the toast, then cook under a preheated medium grill for 3 minutes until golden and bubbling. Serve with a watercress salad.

Cheesy Smoked Mackerel Bites

Mix together 75 g (3 oz) cream cheese, 1 x 150 g (5 oz) smoked mackerel fillet, skin and any bones discarded, and 25 g (1 oz) grated Cheddar. Spread over 4 lightly toasted pieces of bread, sprinkle with a little Tabasco sauce, then cook under a medium grill for 3–5 minutes until golden and bubbling.

Smoked Haddock Rarebit Bake

Heat 200 ml (7 fl oz) ale in a saucepan until boiling. Take off the heat and stir in 300 g (10 oz) grated Cheddar cheese until melted. Lightly beat 2 egg yolks, then beat in 3 tablespoons of the ale mixture. Pour this back into the pan and cook over a low heat for 3–5 minutes until the sauce starts to thicken.

Add a drop of Worcestershire sauce. Place 4 x 150 g (5 oz) smoked haddock fillets in a greased baking dish. Pour over the sauce and top with 1 thinly sliced tomato. Place in a preheated oven, 220°C (425°F), Gas Mark 7, for 15 minutes until golden and the fish is cooked through.

QuickCook
Midweek Dinners

Recipes listed by cooking time

3O **2O**

Baked Red Mullet with Orange and Olive Couscous

Serves 4

4 red mullet fillets, about 150 g (5 oz) each

4 tablespoons olive oil, plus extra for oiling

finely grated rind and juice of 1 orange, plus 1 whole orange

4 thyme sprigs

375 g (12 oz) couscous

400 ml (14 fl oz) hot vegetable stock

finely grated rind and juice of ½ lemon

100 g (3½ oz) radishes, thinly sliced

75 g (3 oz) pitted black olives, chopped

handful of flat leaf parsley, chopped

salt and pepper

- Place the fish fillets on a lightly oiled baking sheet. Season well, then drizzle over 1 tablespoon of the oil and a little of the orange juice and scatter with the thyme sprigs. Place in a preheated oven, 180 °C (350 °F), Gas Mark 4, for 15 minutes until just cooked through.

- Meanwhile, place the couscous in a large bowl. Pour over the hot stock, cover and leave for 5–10 minutes until all the liquid is absorbed and the couscous has swelled. Add the orange and lemon rind with a little more of the orange juice, the lemon juice and the remaining oil, then leave to cool.

- Peel the remaining orange, discarding any white pith, then cut into small pieces and stir through with a fork, breaking up any clumps. Season and add the radishes, olives and parsley just before serving with the fish.

 Red Mullet with Orange and Olive Dressing Heat a griddle pan until smoking hot. Brush 2 tablespoons olive oil over 4 x 125 g (4 oz) red mullet fillets and season well. Cook on the pan for 3–5 minutes until just cooked through. Toss together the finely grated rind of ½ orange, juice of ½ lemon, 3 tablespoons olive oil and 25 g (1 oz) chopped pitted black olives. Spoon over the fish to serve.

 Orange and Olive Baked Red Mullet Season 2 x 250 g (8 oz) whole red mullet, gutted and scaled, and place in a lightly oiled baking dish. Mix together 3 tablespoons olive oil, a good squeeze of lemon juice and the juice of ½ orange. Cut the remaining ½ orange into slices and arrange around the fish along with 4 thyme sprigs. Pour over the dressing. Place in a preheated oven, 180 °C (350 °F), Gas Mark 4, for 15 minutes. Add 75 g (3 oz) pitted black olives and bake for a further 5–10 minutes until the fish is cooked through. Serve one fillet per person.

3⟩ Tuna with Caramelized Onion and Sherry Sauce

Serves 4

3 tablespoons olive oil
2 onions, thinly sliced
2 garlic cloves, crushed
200 ml (7 fl oz) dry sherry
4 tuna steaks, about 175 g
(6 oz) each
salt and pepper
handful of flat leaf parsley,
chopped, to garnish

- Heat 2 tablespoons of the oil in a frying pan. Add the onions and cook over a low heat for 15–20 minutes until soft and starting to turn golden. Add the garlic and cook for 1 minute. Pour over the sherry and simmer for a few minutes until you have a rich sauce. Remove from the pan and set aside. Wipe the pan clean with kitchen paper.

- Heat the remaining oil in the pan and season the tuna steaks well. Add the tuna steaks to the pan and cook for 1–2 minutes on each side until lightly browned. Pour over the onion sauce, then scatter with the parsley and serve immediately.

 Tuna Salad with Sherry Dressing

Whisk together 1 tablespoon sherry vinegar and 3 tablespoons extra virgin olive oil until well blended, then season well. Chop 1 ready-roasted red pepper into strips. Toss with 75 g (3 oz) rocket leaves, 175 g (6 oz) drained canned tuna and the dressing.

 Paprika Tuna with Sherry Dressing

Stir together 3 tablespoons olive oil, 1 tablespoon smoked paprika, the finely chopped leaves from 1 thyme sprig and 1 crushed garlic clove, then season. Spread the mixture over 4 x 175 g (6 oz) tuna steaks and leave to marinate for 10 minutes. Heat a griddle pan until smoking hot.

Brush away the excess marinade from the tuna and cook for 2 minutes on each side until golden on the outside but still rare inside. Whisk together 1 tablespoon sherry vinegar and a little more olive oil. Place the tuna on serving plates, drizzle over the dressing and scatter with some chopped flat leaf parsley to serve.

FIS-MIDW-CAJ

20 Prawn Laksa

Serves 4

1 tablespoon vegetable oil

2 tablespoons laksa curry paste or Thai red curry paste mixed with a pinch of turmeric

400 ml (14 fl oz) chicken stock

400 ml (14 fl oz) coconut milk

1 lemon grass stalk

1 kaffir lime leaf

4 quails' eggs or 2 hens' eggs

125 g (4 oz) dried medium rice noodles

250 g (8 oz) raw large peeled prawns

To serve

bean sprouts

cucumber matchsticks

coriander, chopped

lime wedges

- Heat the oil in a large saucepan. Add the curry paste and cook for 2 minutes. Pour over the stock and coconut milk and add the lemon grass and lime leaf. Leave to simmer for 10 minutes.

- Meanwhile, cook the eggs in boiling water: 4 minutes for quails' eggs or 8 minutes for hens' eggs. Drain and cool under cold running water, then shell and quarter or halve. Cook the noodles according to the pack instructions.

- Remove the lemon grass and lime leaf from the curry. Add the prawns to the pan and cook for 3 minutes until they turn pink and are cooked through, then drain the noodles and stir into the pan. Cook until heated through.

- Ladle into serving bowls. Arrange the eggs on top, then scatter over bean sprouts, cucumber matchsticks, coriander and lime wedges to serve.

 Prawn Cracker Bites

Heat 2 teaspoons vegetable oil in a nonstick frying pan. Add 1 teaspoon laksa or Thai red curry paste and cook for 1 minute. Stir in 100 g (3½ oz) cooked peeled small prawns and heat through. Arrange on top of prawn crackers and top with chopped coriander and a little desiccated coconut.

 Prawn and Sweet Potato Laksa

Wrap 2 teaspoons shrimp paste in foil. Cook in a dry frying pan for 2 minutes on each side. Cool a little, then unwrap the foil and place the paste in a food processor with 1 shallot, 3 red chillies, 2 lemon grass stalks, 2 teaspoons finely chopped fresh root ginger, 25 g (1 oz) macadamia nuts and 2 teaspoons turmeric. Whizz until smooth.

Heat 1 tablespoon vegetable oil in a saucepan. Cook the paste for 2 minutes. Add 400 ml (14 fl oz) each chicken stock and coconut milk. Simmer for 10 minutes. Add 2 peeled and chopped sweet potatoes. Cook for 7 minutes. Add 250 g (8 oz) raw peeled prawns. Cook for 3 minutes until they pink and are cooked through. Serve topped with a handful of bean sprouts and coriander leaves.

30 Seafood Paella

Serves 4

1 tablespoon olive oil

75 g (3 oz) chorizo, thickly sliced

1 onion, finely chopped

1 red pepper, chopped

2 garlic cloves, chopped

300 g (10 oz) paella rice

1 teaspoon smoked paprika

pinch of saffron threads

800 ml (1 pint 7 fl oz) hot chicken stock

300 g (10 oz) cleaned live mussels

8 cooked king prawns, shells on

100 g (3½ oz) raw squid rings

75 g (3 oz) frozen peas

salt and pepper

• Heat the oil in a large, heavy-based saucepan. Add the chorizo to the pan and cook for about 2 minutes until starting to brown. Add the onion and pepper and cook for 3 minutes, then stir in the garlic and cook for 1 minute. Add the rice and stir until well coated.

• Add the paprika and saffron, return the chorizo to the pan, then pour over the hot stock. Bring to the boil, then simmer, uncovered, for 15 minutes. Add the mussels, cover the pan and cook for 3 minutes. Stir in the prawns, squid and peas and cook for a further 2 minutes until the rice is tender (add a drizzle of hot water around the edge of the pan if still a little firm) and the mussels have opened – discard any that remain closed, then serve.

Saffron and Fennel Seafood

Heat 2 tablespoons olive oil in a large saucepan. Cook 1 finely chopped fennel bulb for 2 minutes. Add 150 ml (¼ pint) dry white wine, a good pinch of saffron threads and 500 g (1 lb) cleaned live mussels. Cover and cook for 3 minutes. Add 8 cooked peeled large prawns and 100 g (3½ oz) raw squid rings. Cook for 2 minutes. Discard any mussels that remain closed.

Paella-Style Seafood Pasta

Cook 75 g (3 oz) sliced chorizo in 1 tablespoon olive oil in a large, heavy-based saucepan for 2 minutes. Remove. Add 1 finely chopped onion. Cook for 5 minutes. Add 2 chopped garlic cloves. Cook for 1 minute. Return the chorizo with 1 teaspoon smoked paprika. Add 100 ml (3½ fl oz) dry white wine. Boil for 2 minutes. Add a 200 g (7 oz) can chopped tomatoes and 900 ml (1½ pints) vegetable stock. Bring to the boil. Stir in 300 g (10 oz) angel hair pasta broken into 2.5-cm (1-inch) pieces. Simmer for 7 minutes, stirring often, until nearly cooked through. Add 300 g (10 oz) cleaned live mussels, cover and cook for 3 minutes and discard any that remain closed. Add 8 cooked peeled large prawns and 100 g (3½ oz) raw squid rings. Cook for 2 minutes until the pasta is tender and the seafood is cooked.

 Cajun-Blackened Fish Steaks

Serves 4

50 g (2 oz) butter, melted
4 sea bass fillets, about 175 g
(6 oz) each
2 tablespoons Cajun spice mix
2 teaspoons paprika
salt and pepper

To serve

lime wedges
green salad

- Brush plenty of the melted butter all over the fish fillets and season well. Mix the Cajun spice mix with the paprika and rub all over the fish.

- Heat a large, dry frying pan until smoking hot. Add the sea bass fillets and cook for 1–2 minutes. Turn over and cook for a further 2–3 minutes until the fish is just cooked through and charred all over.

- Drizzle with any remaining butter and serve with lime wedges and a green salad.

 Cajun Fish with Homemade Spice Rub Mix together 1 tablespoon paprika, 1 teaspoon cayenne, ½ teaspoon each dried thyme and oregano, 2 crushed garlic cloves and 2 tablespoons vegetable oil. Make a couple of slashes in the skin of 4 x 200 g (7 oz) red snapper fillets. Rub the spice mix well into the fish and set aside for 5 minutes. Heat a griddle pan until smoking hot and cook for 2–3 minutes on each side until charred and cooked through.

Cajun Fish Stew Melt 40 g (1½ oz) butter in a saucepan. Stir in 40 g (1½ oz) plain flour and cook over a low heat for 10 minutes, or until dark brown. Add 2 teaspoons Cajun spice mix, then slowly whisk in 400 ml (14 fl oz) vegetable stock. Meanwhile, heat 1 tablespoon vegetable oil in a frying pan and cook 1 each chopped onion, green pepper and celery stick for 7 minutes until softened. Add to the saucepan with a 400 g (13 oz) can chopped tomatoes, 1 bay leaf and the leaves from 2 thyme sprigs. Leave to simmer for 10 minutes. Add 300 g (10 oz) skinless monkfish fillet, cut into medallions, and 100 g (3½ oz) raw peeled prawns and cook for 3–5 minutes until cooked through. Serve over plain rice with plenty of Tabasco sauce.

30 Mackerel with Roasted Tomatoes and Horseradish

Serves 4

12 plum tomatoes, halved
3 tablespoons olive oil, plus extra for oiling
1 teaspoon caster sugar
1 teaspoon red wine vinegar
4 mackerel fillets, about 150 g (5 oz) each
150 g (5 oz) crème fraîche
1–2 tablespoons horseradish sauce
75 g (3 oz) rocket leaves
salt and pepper

• Place the tomatoes on a lightly oiled baking sheet. Drizzle over 2 tablespoons of the oil, then sprinkle each tomato half with a little sugar and vinegar. Place in a preheated oven, 200°C (400°F), Gas Mark 6, for 20–25 minutes until browned and soft.

• Meanwhile, heat a large, dry frying pan until hot. Rub the remaining oil over the mackerel and season well. Add the mackerel to the pan, skin-side down, and cook for 5 minutes until the skin is golden. Turn over and cook for a further 3 minutes, or until the fish is cooked through. Stir together the crème fraîche and horseradish sauce.

• Arrange the rocket, roasted tomatoes and mackerel on serving plates and serve with spoonfuls of horseradish sauce on the side.

---

1 **Mackerel and Sunblush Tomato Salad** Gently toss together 100 g (3½ oz) drained canned mackerel in olive oil, 75 g (3 oz) drained sunblush tomatoes and 100 g (3½ oz) rocket leaves. Whisk together the juice of ½ lemon, 3 tablespoons olive oil and 1 tablespoon horseradish sauce. Drizzle over the salad to serve.

2 **Baked Mackerel with Tomatoes** Lightly oil 4 pieces of foil. Take 4 x 150 g (5 oz) mackerel fillets and place one in the centre of each piece of foil, then season. Cover with 2 sliced tomatoes, 1 finely chopped shallot and a handful of flat leaf parsley, chopped, divided between the fillets. Drizzle over more olive oil. Fold the foil over tightly to seal, leaving a little air around the fish. Place on a baking sheet in a preheated oven, 200°C (400°F), Gas Mark 6, for 15 minutes until cooked through. Stir 1 tablespoon horseradish sauce into 4 tablespoons mayonnaise and serve alongside.

1 ⏱ Clams in Black Bean Sauce

Serves 4

2 tablespoons vegetable oil
2 spring onions
2 garlic cloves, crushed
2 teaspoons finely chopped fresh
  root ginger
1 red chilli, finely chopped
1 tablespoon black bean sauce
1 kg (2 lb) cleaned live clams
3 tablespoons chicken stock
1 tablespoon soy sauce
1 tablespoon Shaoxing wine
coriander leaves, to garnish

· Heat the oil in a large saucepan over a high heat. Meanwhile, slice the spring onions and separate the white and green parts. Add the white spring onion, garlic, ginger and chilli to the pan and cook briefly until sizzling. Stir in the black bean sauce, then add the clams and remaining ingredients.

· Cover the pan and cook over a medium heat for 3–5 minutes until the clams have opened. Discard any that remain closed. Divide on to serving plates and scatter over the green spring onion and coriander leaves to serve.

2 ⏱ Mussels in Black Bean Sauce

Rinse 1 tablespoon fermented black beans. Mash with a little sugar. Briefly cook 2 sliced spring onions, 2 crushed garlic cloves and 2 teaspoons each finely chopped fresh root ginger and red chilli in 2 tablespoons hot vegetable oil in a saucepan. Add the beans, 3 tablespoons chicken stock and 2 tablespoons each soy sauce and Shaoxing wine. Bring to the boil, then simmer for 5 minutes. Meanwhile, heat 2 tablespoons oil in another pan. Cook 1 kg (2 lb) cleaned live mussels with 3 tablespoons hot water, covered, for 3–5 minutes until opened. Discard any that remain closed and the top shells. Drizzle over the sauce.

3 ⏱ Sea Bass in Black Bean Sauce

Place a 625 g (1¼ lb) whole sea bass, gutted and scaled, in a heatproof dish. Pour over 50 ml (2 fl oz) Shaoxing wine and add 1 tablespoon fresh root ginger, cut into matchsticks. Place in a steamer, cover and cook for 15 minutes, or until cooked through. Pour away the poaching liquid and keep warm. Heat 1 tablespoon vegetable oil in a frying pan or wok over a high heat. Stir-fry 2 crushed garlic cloves, 1 tablespoon finely chopped fresh root ginger and 2 chopped spring onions for a few seconds. Add 100 g (3½ oz) minced pork and stir-fry for about 2 minutes until starting to turn golden. Pour over 200 ml (7 fl oz) chicken stock and 2 tablespoons each black bean sauce, soy sauce and Shaoxing wine. Cook for about 5 minutes until the pork is cooked through. Mix 1 teaspoon cornflour with 1 tablespoon water and add to the pan. Cook, stirring, until slightly thickened. Pour over the fish and scatter with chopped coriander.

30 Leek and Smoked Haddock Risotto

Serves 4

400 g (13 oz) smoked
  haddock fillet
900 ml (1½ pints) hot
  vegetable stock
25 g (1 oz) butter
1 tablespoon vegetable oil
1 large leek, thickly sliced
300 g (10 oz) risotto rice
100 ml (3½ fl oz) dry white wine
100 g (3½ oz) mascarpone cheese
handful of chives, chopped,
  to garnish
salt

- Place the haddock in a shallow bowl. Pour over the hot stock and leave for 5 minutes until nearly cooked through. Strain the stock through a sieve into a saucepan and keep hot. Break the fish into large flakes, discarding the skin and any bones.

- Meanwhile, heat the butter and oil in a large frying pan. Add the leek and a splash of water, cover and leave to gently cook for 7 minutes, stirring occasionally, until soft. Stir in the rice until well coated, then pour in the wine and cook for 2 minutes until nearly boiled away.

- Add the reserved hot stock, a ladleful at a time, stirring and simmering after each addition until the stock is absorbed before adding the next. After about 15 minutes when all the stock is absorbed and the rice is nearly cooked, add the fish and cook for a further 2 minutes until the rice is tender and still very moist. Stir in the mascarpone and season with salt. Cover and leave to stand for 2 minutes.

- Spoon into serving bowls and scatter with the chives.

---

10 Leek-Crusted Haddock Fillets

Cook 1 large, very thinly sliced leek in boiling water for 4 minutes. Drain well. Meanwhile, cook 4 x 150 g (5 oz) thin haddock fillets, skin-side up, under a preheated hot grill for 3 minutes. Mix the leek with 75 g (3 oz) grated Cheddar cheese. Turn the fish over, scatter over the leek mixture and cook for a further 3–5 minutes until golden and bubbling and the fish is just cooked through.

20 Smoked Haddock, Leek and Potato Soup

Soup Heat 25 g (1 oz) butter and 1 tablespoon vegetable oil in a large saucepan. Add 1 large, thinly sliced leek and a splash of water, cover and gently cook for 5 minutes, stirring occasionally. Meanwhile, place 400 g (13 oz) smoked haddock fillets in a shallow bowl. Pour over 900 ml (1½ pints) hot vegetable stock. Leave for 5 minutes. Strain the stock into the pan. Add 1 peeled and diced potato. Simmer for about 12 minutes until the potato is soft, then mash slightly. Break the fish into large chunks, discarding the skin and any bones. Add to the pan with about 200 ml (7 fl oz) milk. Heat through. Scatter with some chopped chives before serving.

Hake with Spicy Coriander Pesto

Serves 4

75 ml (3 fl oz) olive oil
4 hake steaks, about 175 g (6 oz) each
2 green chillies
2 red chillies
4 cardamom seeds, ground
1 teaspoon caraway seeds, ground
1 garlic clove, crushed
bunch of coriander
squeeze of lemon juice
salt and pepper

To serve

chopped cucumber
pitta bread

- Heat a griddle pan until hot. Brush 1 tablespoon of the oil over the fish steaks and season well with salt and pepper. Add the fish to the pan and cook for 3–5 minutes on each side until just cooked through.

- Meanwhile, place the remaining oil with all the other remaining ingredients in a small food processor and whizz until you have a smooth paste.

- Spoon the pesto over the fish and serve with a cucumber salad and pitta bread.

 Hake with Coriander and Coconut Sauce

Heat 1 tablespoon vegetable oil in a saucepan. Cook 1 finely chopped shallot for 5 minutes. Stir in 1 teaspoon finely chopped fresh root ginger, 4 ground cardamom seeds and 1 finely chopped red chilli. Cook for 2 minutes. Pour over 100 ml (3½ fl oz) coconut milk and 200 ml (7 fl oz) vegetable stock. Add 1 each kaffir lime leaf and lemon grass stalk, 1 tablespoon fish sauce and a pinch of caster sugar. Simmer for 10 minutes. Stir through a large handful of coriander, chopped. Meanwhile, cook the hake fillets as above. Spoon over the sauce, discarding the lime leaf and lemon grass.

 Fish Soup with Coriander Pesto

Heat 2 tablespoons vegetable oil in a saucepan. Cook 1 finely chopped onion for 7 minutes until very soft. Add 2 crushed garlic cloves and 1 teaspoon finely chopped fresh root ginger and cook for 2 minutes. Stir in 2 teaspoons ground cumin, 1 teaspoon ground coriander and ½ teaspoon ground fennel. Pour in 1.5 litres (2½ pints) water and bring to the boil. Add a rinsed and drained 400 g (13 oz) can chickpeas and simmer for 10 minutes. Scoop out and reserve a handful of chickpeas, then whizz the soup in a food processor until smooth. Return to the pan with the whole chickpeas and 2 x 175 g (6 oz) skinless white fish fillets, such as hake. Cook for about 7 minutes until the fish flakes. Meanwhile, in a small food processor, whizz together the finely grated rind of 1 lime, a squeeze of lime juice, 1 chopped red chilli, a large handful of coriander and 5–6 tablespoons vegetable oil. Drizzle over the soup to serve.

30 Spicy Peanut and Fish Stew

Serves 4

1 tablespoon vegetable oil
1 onion, finely chopped
2 garlic cloves, crushed
1 teaspoon finely chopped fresh
  root ginger
1 teaspoon ground coriander
pinch of freshly grated nutmeg
pinch of cayenne
400 g (13 oz) can chopped
  tomatoes
50 g (2 oz) peanut butter
4 coley fillets, about
  175 g (6 oz) each, skin on and
  cut into large chunks
squeeze of lime juice

To serve

25 g (1 oz) roasted peanuts,
  roughly chopped
coriander
cooked plain rice

- Heat the oil in a large saucepan. Add the onion and cook for 5 minutes until softened. Stir in the garlic and ginger and cook for 1 minute. Add the spices and cook for 1–2 minutes, then stir in the tomatoes and peanut butter. Top up with a little water and leave to simmer for 15 minutes.

- Add the fish to the pan and cook for a further 5 minutes until just cooked through. Season and add the lime juice, then serve scattered with chopped coriander and peanuts and plain boiled rice.

---

10 Spicy Peanut Fish Strips

Mix together 5 tablespoons peanut butter, 1 tablespoon soy sauce and a pinch of caster sugar. Cut 350 g (11½ oz) skinless firm white fish fillets, such as cod, into strips. Brush with the peanut mixture, then drizzle over a little vegetable oil. Cook under a preheated hot grill for 3 minutes on each side until just cooked through. Serve with lime wedges.

20 Fish in Peanut and Coconut Curry

Sauce Heat 2 teaspoons vegetable oil in a saucepan. Cook 1 finely chopped shallot for 3–5 minutes until softened. Stir in 1 tablespoon Thai red curry paste and 2 teaspoons finely chopped fresh root ginger. Pour over 100 ml (3½ fl oz) coconut milk, 200 ml (7 fl oz) hot vegetable stock and 1 tablespoon fish sauce. Add 1 lemon grass stalk and 1 kaffir lime leaf.

Leave to simmer for 5–10 minutes, then stir in 3 tablespoons peanut butter. Meanwhile, heat 1 tablespoon vegetable oil in a large, nonstick frying pan. Pat 4 x 150 g (5 oz) skinless coley fillets dry with kitchen paper and season. Cook for 3–5 minutes on each side until just cooked through. Spoon over the sauce to serve.

 # Skate with Lemon Butter and Capers

Serves 2

75 g (3 oz) butter
4 skate wings, about 250 g (8 oz) each
juice of 1 lemon
3 tablespoons drained capers
salt and pepper

- Heat the butter in a large, nonstick frying pan until melted and starting to turn brown. Season the skate wings and add to the pan along with the capers. Cook for 3 minutes on each side until lightly browned and just cooked through. Transfer the skate to serving plates and spoon over the capers.

- Stir the lemon juice and capers through the butter in the pan, then drizzle over the skate.

 ## Poached Skate with Black Butter

Place 2 x 250 g (8 oz) skate wings in a large saucepan with 75 ml (3 fl oz) dry white wine and 1 bay leaf. Pour over enough water to cover and then very gently poach for 10–15 minutes until just cooked through. Remove the skate and keep warm. Heat 50 g (2 oz) butter in a small saucepan until it turns dark brown, watching carefully. Take off the heat and stir in 3 tablespoons drained capers and a handful of flat leaf parsley, chopped. Spoon over the fish and serve with lemon wedges.

 ## Skate with Buttery Lemon Onions

Heat 2 tablespoons olive oil and 3 tablespoons butter in a frying pan. Cook 1 sliced onion over a low heat for 15 minutes until very soft. Add a pinch of sugar and cook for a further 5 minutes until well browned. Leave to cool a little, then stir in a good squeeze of lemon juice, the finely grated rind of ½ lemon and a large handful of flat leaf parsley, chopped. Meanwhile, heat 1 tablespoon olive oil in a large frying pan and cook 2 x 250 g (8 oz) skate wings for 3 minutes on each side until just cooked through. Serve with the onions.

Baked Sea Bream with Fennel

Serves 4

3 tablespoons olive oil, plus extra
  for oiling
4 small fennel bulbs, quartered
1 shallot, thinly sliced
1 garlic clove, sliced
4 sea bream, about 625 g (1¼ lb)
  each, gutted and scaled
juice of ½ lemon
handful of oregano leaves
salt and pepper

- Heat 2 tablespoons of the oil in a saucepan and cook the fennel and shallot for 5 minutes until softened. Stir in the garlic and cook for a further 1 minute. Transfer the fennel mixture to a lightly oiled roasting tray and arrange the fish on top. Season, then squeeze over the lemon juice and drizzle over the remaining oil. Sprinkle with a little of the oregano and cover with foil.

- Place in a preheated oven, 200°C (400°F), Gas Mark 6, for 10 minutes. Remove the foil and bake for a further 5–10 minutes until the fish is cooked through.

- Transfer to a serving plate, scatter over the remaining oregano and serve.

 Fennel Salad with Seared Sea Bream

Heat a griddle pan until smoking hot. Rub 1 tablespoon olive oil over 4 x 175 g (6 oz) sea bream fillets, then season. Cook, skin-side down, for 5 minutes. Turn over and cook for a further 3 minutes until cooked through. Meanwhile, use a very sharp knife to slice 1 large fennel bulb as thinly as you can. Toss with the juice of ½ lemon, 3 tablespoons olive oil and a handful of flat leaf parsley, chopped. Serve with the fish.

Grilled Whole Sea Bream

Using a sharp knife, make 3 shallow slashes across either side of 4 x 625 g (1¼ lb) sea bream, gutted and scaled. Mix together 1 teaspoon crushed fennel seeds, the finely grated rind of 1 lemon and a handful of oregano leaves, chopped. Stir in 3 tablespoons olive oil. Rub all over the fish inside and out. Cook on a hot barbecue or under a preheated hot grill for about 8 minutes on each side until a little charred and cooked through. Squeeze over the juice of 1 lemon and serve.

Tuna Teriyaki with Wasabi Mash

Serves 4

750 g (1½ lb) potatoes, peeled
and quartered
1 tablespoon vegetable oil
4 tuna steaks, about 150 g
(5 oz) each
5 tablespoons soy sauce
2 tablespoons rice vinegar
2 tablespoons soft brown sugar
5 tablespoons crème fraîche
1 tablespoon wasabi paste
salt and pepper
steamed sugar snap peas, to
serve (optional)

- Cook the potatoes in a saucepan of boiling water for 12–15 minutes until soft.

- Meanwhile, brush the oil all over the tuna steaks. Heat a griddle pan until smoking hot. Add the tuna and cook for 2–3 minutes on each side for medium-rare. While the tuna is cooking, heat the soy sauce, vinegar and sugar in a small saucepan for about 2 minutes until warmed and slightly syrupy. Mix together the crème fraîche and wasabi.

- Drain the potatoes and mash until smooth, then stir through the wasabi mixture. Season well. Spoon the mash on to warmed serving plates along with the tuna. Drizzle over the warm sauce and serve with some steamed sugar snap peas, if you like.

 Tuna with Wasabi Butter

Mix together 50 g (2 oz) softened butter and 2 teaspoons wasabi paste. Season 4 x 150 g (5 oz) tuna steaks. Cook on a smoking hot griddle pan for 2–3 minutes on each side for medium-rare. Top with the butter before serving.

 Tuna Skewers with Wasabi Mayo

Mix together 5 tablespoons soy sauce and 2 tablespoons each rice vinegar and soft brown sugar until the sugar has dissolved. Cut 4 x 150 g (5 oz) tuna steaks into bite-sized pieces, pour over the soy sauce mixture and leave to marinate for 20 minutes. Meanwhile, mix together 100 ml (3½ fl oz) mayonnaise and 1 tablespoon wasabi paste.

Place in a dipping bowl. Remove the tuna from the marinade and lightly pat dry with kitchen paper. Place some mixed white and black sesame seeds on a plate. Thread the tuna pieces on to metal skewers, then roll in the sesame seeds to coat. Drizzle with a little vegetable oil. Cook under a preheated hot grill for about 2 minutes on each side until golden. Serve with the mayonnaise for dipping.

Monkfish, Chorizo and Chickpea Stew

Serves 4

2 tablespoons olive oil

100 g (3½ oz) chorizo, thickly sliced

3 garlic cloves, sliced

1 tablespoon tomato purée

50 ml (2 fl oz) dry white wine

200 g (7 oz) can chopped tomatoes

400 g (13 oz) can chickpeas, rinsed and drained

375 g (12 oz) skinless monkfish fillet, cut into bite-sized pieces

200 g (7 oz) baby spinach leaves

salt and pepper

- Heat the oil in a large saucepan. Add the chorizo and cook for about 2 minutes until starting to brown, then add the garlic and cook for 1 minute. Stir in the tomato purée and the wine and cook until nearly boiled away. Add the tomatoes and chickpeas and leave to simmer for 10 minutes, topping up with water if necessary.

- Add the monkfish to the pan and cook for 5 minutes, or until just cooked through. Gently stir in the spinach and season, then serve.

 Chorizo Monkfish with Chickpea Mash

Heat 1 tablespoon olive oil in a frying pan. Cook 450 g (14½ oz) skinless monkfish fillet, cut into bite-sized pieces and seasoned, for 5 minutes, turning occasionally, until cooked through. Add 4 thin slices of chorizo for the last minute of cooking to crisp and brown. Meanwhile, boil 2 x 400 g (13 oz) cans chickpeas for 1 minute. Drain and mash with 3 tablespoons crème fraîche, a squeeze of lemon juice and some chopped flat leaf parsley. Serve with the fish, chopped tomatoes and lemon wedges.

 Chickpea Pancakes with Monkfish and Chorizo Beat together 150 g (5 oz) chickpea (gram) flour, 250 ml (8 fl oz) water and a good pinch of salt until smooth. Leave to rest for 15 minutes. Meanwhile, heat 2 tablespoons vegetable oil in a saucepan. Add 1 sliced onion and 100 g (3½ oz) thickly sliced chorizo and cook for 2 minutes. Add 375 g (12 oz) skinless monkfish fillet, cut into bite-sized pieces, and cook for 3 minutes. Turn over, then add 2 sliced garlic cloves and 100 g (3½ oz) halved cherry tomatoes and cook for about 2 minutes until the fish is cooked through and the tomatoes have wilted. Keep warm. Heat 1 teaspoon oil in a large, nonstick frying pan. Add a ladleful of the batter, swirl around the pan and cook for 1–2 minutes. Turn over with a fish slice and cook for 1 minute more. Keep warm between 2 plates and repeat with the remaining batter to make a further 3 pancakes. Spoon a little of the fish mixture on to the pancakes and scatter over some coriander leaves to serve.

30 Baked Sea Bass with Romesco Salad

Serves 3–4

1.5 kg (3 lb) whole sea bass, gutted and scaled
6 tablespoons olive oil
3 thyme sprigs
pinch of chilli flakes
1 lemon, sliced
3 red peppers
50 g (2 oz) blanched almonds
25 g (1 oz) blanched hazelnuts
1 tablespoon sherry vinegar
1 crushed garlic clove
½ teaspoon smoked paprika
2 plum tomatoes, chopped
handful of flat leaf parsley, chopped
salt and pepper

• Using a sharp knife, make 3 shallow slashes across either side of the sea bass. Mix together 2 tablespoons of the oil, the thyme and chilli. Rub all over the fish. Place in a baking dish and arrange the lemon slices around. Bake in a preheated oven, 220°C (425°F), Gas Mark 7, for 20–25 minutes until just cooked through.

• Meanwhile, rub 1 tablespoon of the remaining oil over the peppers, place in a baking dish and cook in the oven with the fish for 15–20 minutes until well browned. Transfer to a sealed freezer bag for 5 minutes. Peel away the skins, discard the cores and seeds and chop.

• While the fish and peppers are cooking, heat a small, dry saucepan and cook the nuts for 3 minutes until lightly browned. Leave to cool a little, then roughly chop. Whisk together the vinegar, garlic and paprika. Add the remaining oil and season well. Toss with the peppers, tomatoes, nuts and parsley. Serve the baked fish with the Romesco salad.

---

 10 Seafood Skewers with Romesco Sauce Heat a griddle pan until hot. Thread 12 each of cooked peeled large prawns and cleaned scallops on to metal skewers. Drizzle over 1 tablespoon olive oil and cook on the pan for 3 minutes on each side until just cooked through. Meanwhile, in a small food processor, whizz together 2 ready-roasted red peppers, 50 g (2 oz) toasted almonds, 3 tablespoons olive oil, 2 teaspoons sherry vinegar and ½ teaspoon smoked paprika. Serve with the skewers for dipping.

 20 Romesco Seafood Stew Heat 3 tablespoons olive oil in a large saucepan. Add 1 finely chopped onion and cook for 2 minutes. Stir in 2 sliced red peppers and cook for a further 5 minutes until softened. Stir in 2 crushed garlic cloves and the finely chopped leaves from 1 rosemary sprig. Add 1 teaspoon tomato purée and ½ teaspoon smoked paprika, followed by 100 ml (3½ fl oz) dry white wine. Boil for 1 minute until reduced, then pour over a 400 g (13 oz) can chopped tomatoes. Bring to the boil, then simmer for 5 minutes. Add 500 g (1 lb) cleaned live clams and 250 g (8 oz) raw peeled large prawns and cook for 3 minutes. Stir in 75 g (3 oz) toasted and roughly ground almonds. Cook for a further 2 minutes until thickened and the seafood is cooked through, discarding any clams that remain closed. Scatter with chopped flat leaf parsley to serve.

Seared Gurnard with Tapenade and White Bean Mash

Serves 4

2 tablespoons olive oil
1 shallot, chopped
1 garlic clove, crushed
2 x 400 g (13 oz) cans cannellini
  beans, rinsed and drained
150 ml (¼ pint) vegetable or
  chicken stock
4 gurnard fillets, about 150 g
  (5 oz) each
salt and pepper

For the tapenade

1 x 50 g (2 oz) can anchovy
  fillets in olive oil
1 crushed garlic clove
2 tablespoons drained capers
100 g (3½ oz) pitted black olives
grated rind and juice of ½ lemon
large handful of flat leaf parsley

- Heat 1 tablespoon of the oil in a saucepan. Add the shallot and cook for 5–7 minutes until softened. Stir in the garlic and cook for a further 1 minute. Add the beans and stock and leave to simmer for 5 minutes. Whizz in a food processor until smooth. Return to the pan and keep warm.

- Meanwhile, heat the remaining oil in a large, nonstick frying pan. Season the gurnard, add to the pan, skin-side down, and cook for 5 minutes until golden. Turn over and cook for a further 3–5 minutes until the fish is cooked through.

- While the fish is cooking, drain the oil from the anchovies and reserve. Roughly chop the anchovies with all the other tapenade ingredients and mix with the reserved anchovy oil until you have a coarse sauce.

- Place the bean mash on a plate, top with the fish and then drizzle over the tapenade.

 Seared Gurnard with Smashed Beans

Cook the gurnard as above. Meanwhile, boil 2 rinsed and drained 400 g (13 oz) cans cannellini beans for 2 minutes. Drain. Roughly mash with 4 tablespoons olive oil. Stir in 25 g (1 oz) chopped pitted black olives, 2 finely chopped anchovies, 1 thinly sliced spring onion and plenty of chopped flat leaf parsley. Serve with the fish.

 Baked Beans with Seared Gurnard

Cook 1 chopped shallot in 1 tablespoon olive oil for 5–7 minutes. Add 1 crushed garlic clove. Cook for 1 minute. Add 2 rinsed and drained 400 g (13 oz) cans cannellini beans and 150 ml (¼ pint) vegetable stock. Simmer for 5 minutes. Stir in 6 tablespoons crème fraîche. Spoon into a baking dish and cover with 50 g (2 oz) dried breadcrumbs. Place in a preheated oven, 200°C (400°F), Gas Mark 6, for 15 minutes. Meanwhile, cook the gurnard as above. While the fish is cooking, mix together 100 g (3½ oz) pitted black olives, 200 g (7 oz) halved cherry tomatoes, 3 tablespoons olive oil and 2 teaspoons each capers and red wine vinegar. Season. Spoon over the fish and serve with the beans.

FIS-MIDW-XOI

 # Grilled Red Mullet with Yogurt Dill Sauce

Serves 4

4 red mullet fillets, about 150 g (5 oz) each
2 tablespoons olive oil
5 tablespoons natural yogurt
juice of ½ lemon
2 garlic cloves, crushed
handful of dill, finely chopped
salt and pepper
grilled courgettes, to serve

- Season the fish fillets, then rub all over with 1 tablespoon of the oil. Cook in griddle pan over a high heat for 5 minutes. Turn over and cook for a further 3–5 minutes until just cooked through.

- Meanwhile, mix together the remaining oil, yogurt, lemon juice, garlic and dill, then season.

- Spoon the sauce over the fish and serve with grilled courgettes.

 ### Red Mullet with Tahini Yogurt Sauce

Heat 1 tablespoon olive oil and cook 1 small finely chopped onion for 7 minutes until softened. Add 2 crushed garlic cloves and cook for 2 minutes. Stir in a handful of coriander, chopped, and sizzle for a couple of seconds, then add a pinch of cayenne, the juice of ½ lemon and 3 tablespoons tahini paste. Stir until you have a smooth paste. Take off the heat and slowly stir in 5 tablespoons natural yogurt. Cook the red mullet as above. Spoon over the sauce to serve.

 ### Indian Yogurt-Baked Haddock

Mix together 300 ml (½ pint) natural yogurt, 2 tablespoons ground coriander, 2 teaspoons ground cumin, 1 finely chopped green chilli and 1 teaspoon finely chopped fresh root ginger. Place 4 x 175 g (6 oz) thick haddock fillets in an oiled baking dish. Season and pour over the yogurt mixture. Cut 40 g (1½ oz) butter into small pieces and dot over the fish. Cover with foil and place in a preheated oven, 190°C (375°F), Gas Mark 5, for 20 minutes until just cooked through. Transfer the fish to a serving plate. Stir a little more melted butter into the yogurt if it has split, then scatter with chopped coriander and serve.

Halibut with Peas and Lettuce

Serves 4

40 g (1½ oz) butter
2 tablespoons olive oil
2 shallots, finely chopped
50 g (2 oz) lardons
300 g (10 oz) frozen peas
150 ml (¼ pint) hot chicken stock
5 tablespoons crème fraîche
2 Little Gem lettuces
4 halibut steaks, about 175 g
   (6 oz) each
squeeze of lemon juice
salt and pepper

- Heat 1 tablespoon of the butter and 1 tablespoon of the oil in a saucepan. Add the shallots and lardons and cook over a low heat for 7–10 minutes until very soft. Stir in the peas and stock and simmer for about 5 minutes. Stir in the crème fraîche and season with salt and pepper. Roughly chop the lettuce and toss around the pan for 1 minute to coat in the juices.

- Meanwhile, heat the remaining oil in a frying pan. Pat the fish dry with kitchen paper and season with salt. Cook for 5 minutes on each side until just cooked through. Add the remaining butter to the pan along with the lemon juice and swirl around until the butter has melted.

- Serve the fish with the peas and lettuce together with some new potatoes, if liked.

Halibut with Pea and Mint Salad

Heat 1 tablespoon olive oil in a frying pan. Pat 4 x 175 g (6 oz) halibut steaks dry and season with salt. Cook for 5 minutes on each side until just cooked through. Meanwhile, boil 300 g (10 oz) frozen peas for 3 minutes. Drain and cool under the cold tap. Whisk together a good squeeze of lemon juice and 3 tablespoons extra virgin olive oil. Season and toss through the peas with a handful of mint leaves, chopped. Serve alongside the halibut.

 ### Halibut Baked in Lettuce Leaves

Separate 8 large leaves from a Cos lettuce and trim away any thick stems. Place in a shallow dish, pour over boiling water and leave for 2 minutes until softened. Drain and cool under the cold tap. Remove any bones from 4 x 175 g (6 oz) halibut steaks and season. Place each piece of fish on top of a lettuce leaf with a handful of dill, then fold over to cover (add another leaf if it doesn't quite fit) and tuck the ends underneath. Heat 15 g (½ oz) butter and 1 tablespoon olive oil in an ovenproof frying pan and cook the fish, seam-side down, for 1 minute. Pour over 100 ml (3½ fl oz) dry white wine and dot with a little more butter. Place in a preheated oven, 160°C (325°F), Gas Mark 3, for 15–20 minutes until just cooked through. Serve with boiled new potatoes and peas.

Coley Wrapped in Parma Ham with Lentil Salad

Serves 4

325 g (11 oz) dried Puy lentils

4 skinless coley fillets, about 150 g (5 oz) each

4 slices of Parma ham

5 tablespoons olive oil

2 tablespoons red wine vinegar

1 garlic clove, crushed

2 spring onions, chopped

100 g (3½ oz) baby spinach leaves

3 plum tomatoes, chopped

salt and pepper

- Rinse the lentils, then drain, place in a saucepan and cover with twice their volume of boiling water. Simmer for 15 minutes, or until just tender.

- Meanwhile, season the fish fillets, then halve each slice of Parma ham and roughly wrap around each fillet. Heat a frying pan, add 1 tablespoon of the oil and cook the fish for 2 minutes until lightly browned on the underside. Drizzle another tablespoon of the oil over the fish. Place the pan under a preheated hot grill, making sure you turn the handle away from the heat if not flameproof, and cook for 5–7 minutes until just cooked through. Mix together the remaining oil, vinegar and garlic.

- Cool the lentils a little under the cold tap, then drain. Toss through the spring onions, spinach and tomatoes, then stir through the dressing. Serve alongside the fish.

 Prawn, Lentil and Parma Ham Salad

Rinse and drain a 400 g (13 oz) can lentils. Mix together 3 tablespoons olive oil, 2 tablespoons red wine vinegar and 1 crushed garlic clove and stir through. Heat 2 teaspoons olive oil in a nonstick frying pan and cook 4 slices of Parma ham for about 1 minute until just crisp. Toss 200 g (7 oz) cooked peeled prawns through the lentils with 75 g (3 oz) drained sunblush tomatoes and 50 g (2 oz) spinach leaves. Scatter the Parma ham over the top.

 Lentil and Smoked Haddock Pilaff

Pour boiling water over 400 g (13 oz) smoked haddock fillet in a shallow saucepan to cover and gently cook for about 7 minutes, or until the fish flakes easily. Meanwhile, heat 15 g (½ oz) butter and 2 tablespoons vegetable oil in a frying pan. Cook 1 finely chopped onion for 5–7 minutes until soft. Stir in 2 crushed garlic cloves, 2 teaspoons finely chopped fresh root ginger and 325 g (11 oz) basmati rice. Cook, stirring, for 1 minute, then add 1 teaspoon each ground cumin and coriander and a pinch of turmeric. Lift out the fish, discard the skin and any bones and break into large flakes. Top the poaching water up to 1 litre (1¾ pints). Pour over the rice mixture. Add 75 g (3 oz) rinsed and drained dried red lentils. Bring to the boil, then cover and cook for 15 minutes. Add 75 g (3 oz) frozen peas and the fish. Cook for another 5 minutes until the peas and rice are tender. Scatter over chopped coriander to serve.

30 Thai Green Curry with Monkfish and Tomatoes

Serves 4

2 tablespoons Thai green curry
paste
handful coriander
1 tablespoon vegetable oil
300 ml (½ pint) fish or chicken
stock
400 ml (14 fl oz) coconut milk
2 tablespoons fish sauce
2 teaspoons soft brown sugar
500 g (1 lb) skinless monkfish
fillet, cut into 2.5-cm (1-inch)
cubes
75 g (3 oz) cherry tomatoes,
halved
handful of basil, chopped, to
garnish

- Put the Thai green curry paste and coriander in a mini food processor and whizz to a smooth paste.

- Heat the oil in a large saucepan. Add the curry paste and stir around the pan for 3–5 minutes until the oil starts to separate. Pour over the stock and coconut milk and bring to the boil. Add the fish sauce and sugar and leave to simmer for 10 minutes.

- Stir in the monkfish and tomatoes and cook for a further 7–10 minutes until just cooked through. Scatter over the basil and serve.

 Monkfish with Green Curry Sauce

Cook 1 tablespoon Thai green curry paste in 1 tablespoon vegetable oil for 1–2 minutes. Add 100 ml (3½ fl oz) coconut milk, bring to the boil, then simmer. Meanwhile, cook 500 g (1 lb) skinless monkfish fillet, cut into 1.5-cm (¾-inch) thick medallions and seasoned, in 1 tablespoon vegetable oil in a large, nonstick frying pan for 2–3 minutes on each side. Stir some chopped coriander into the sauce. Pour over the fish.

 Monkfish Thai Green Curry

Heat 2 tablespoons vegetable oil in a large saucepan. Add 2 tablespoons Thai green curry paste and cook for 3 minutes until the oil starts to separate. Pour over 300 ml (½ pint) fish or chicken stock, 400 ml (14 fl oz) coconut milk, 2 tablespoons fish sauce and 2 teaspoons soft brown sugar. Simmer for 10 minutes. Add 150 g (5 oz) green beans and cook for 1–2 minutes. Stir in 500 g (1 lb) skinless monkfish fillet, cut into

2.5-cm (1-inch) cubes, and cook for 3–5 minutes. Scatter over a handful of basil leaves to serve.

Peppered Tuna with Rocket and Parmesan

Serves 4

5 tablespoons extra virgin olive oil

400 g (13 oz) very fresh tuna steak

1 tablespoon black peppercorns, coarsely crushed

1 tablespoon balsamic vinegar

100 g (3½ oz) wild rocket leaves

salt

Parmesan cheese shavings, to serve

- Brush 1 tablespoon of the oil over the tuna. Place the crushed peppercorns on a plate, then roll the tuna in the pepper until well coated. Wrap up tightly in a piece of foil. Heat a dry, heavy-based frying pan until smoking hot. Add the wrapped tuna to the pan and cook for 7 minutes, turning every minute or so to cook evenly on each side. Remove from the pan and leave to cool a little.

- Whisk the remaining oil with the vinegar until well combined, then season with salt. Just before serving, unwrap the tuna and slice. Toss the rocket with the dressing and arrange on serving plates. Scatter over the tuna and sprinkle with Parmesan shavings to serve.

 Rocket and Tuna Pasta Salad

Cook 325 g (11 oz) quick-cook penne according to the pack instructions. Drain and cool under the cold tap. Meanwhile, mix together 4 tablespoons mayonnaise, 100 g (3½ oz) drained canned tuna and plenty of pepper. Stir into the pasta, then toss through 50 g (2 oz) rocket leaves and serve.

 Slow-Cooked Tuna with Rocket Pesto

Rub 1 tablespoon olive oil over 4 x 175 g (6 oz) thick tuna steaks, place on a baking sheet and season well. Place in a preheated oven, 110°C (225°F), Gas Mark ¼, for 25 minutes. Meanwhile, in a food processor, whizz together 100 g (3½ oz) rocket leaves, 2 tablespoons grated Parmesan cheese and a good squeeze of lemon juice. Stir in 5 tablespoons olive oil and 1 teaspoon drained capers and spoon over the tuna to serve.

20 Pad Thai

Serves 4

200 g (7 oz) dried medium rice
noodles

2 tablespoons vegetable oil

2 eggs, beaten

200 g (7 oz) raw large prawns,
tails on

2 garlic cloves, crushed

2 teaspoons tamarind paste
(optional)

½ teaspoon chilli flakes

2 tablespoons soft brown sugar

2 tablespoons fish sauce

3 spring onions, sliced

50 g (2 oz) bean sprouts

juice of ½ lime

25 g (1 oz) roasted peanuts,
roughly chopped

coriander, chopped, to garnish

- Cook the rice noodles according to the pack instructions.

- Meanwhile, heat a large wok or frying pan and add the oil. Add the eggs and leave to cook for 30 seconds, then stir and break up into small pieces. Add the prawns, garlic, tamarind paste, if using, and chilli flakes and cook for a further 30 seconds. Then add the sugar and fish sauce and cook for a couple of seconds.

- Drain the noodles well and stir into the pan along with the spring onions and bean sprouts. Toss around the pan to heat through, then pour over the lime juice. Spoon on to serving plates and sprinkle over the peanuts. Scatter over the chopped coriander to serve.

Fast Pad Thai with Tofu

Heat 2 tablespoons vegetable oil in a large wok or frying pan. Add 2 beaten eggs, then 2 crushed garlic cloves and ½ teaspoon chilli flakes. Cook for 30 seconds, then stir to break up. Add 300 g (10 oz) straight-to-wok noodles, 2 tablespoons each brown sugar and fish sauce and a splash of water. Cook for 1 minute. Add 75 g (3 oz) bean sprouts, 150 g (5 oz) each cubed tofu and cooked peeled prawns and a squeeze of lime juice. Heat through to serve.

Pad Thai Rice Pot

Heat 2 tablespoons vegetable oil in a saucepan. Add 1 finely chopped onion and cook for 5 minutes until softened. Add 2 teaspoons finely chopped fresh root ginger and 2 crushed garlic cloves and cook for a further 1 minute. Stir in 1 heaped tablespoon Thai green curry paste. Add 300 g (10 oz) jasmine rice, then pour over 750 ml (1¼ pints) vegetable or fish stock and 200 ml (7 fl oz) coconut milk. Season and bring to the boil, then leave to simmer for 15 minutes. Stir in 200 g (7 oz) raw peeled large prawns and 150 g (5 oz) mangetout. Cook for 3–5 minutes until the prawns turn pink and are cooked through. Squeeze over the juice of ½ lime and scatter with plenty of chopped coriander and some chopped roasted peanuts.

Baked Plaice with Cider and Mussel Sauce

Serves 4

25 g (1 oz) butter, plus extra
    for greasing
2 plaice fillets, about 200 g (7 oz)
    each, halved
200 ml (7 fl oz) dry cider
1 shallot, finely chopped
500 g (1 lb) cleaned live mussels
4 tablespoons crème fraîche
handful of flat leaf parsley,
    chopped
salt

- Rub a little butter over the inside of a baking dish, then place the fish fillets in the dish and season with salt. Dot over about half the butter, then pour over a couple of tablespoons of the cider. Cover loosely with a sheet of nonstick baking paper, then place in a preheated oven, 180°C (350°F), Gas Mark 4, for 12–15 minutes until just cooked through.

- Meanwhile, heat the remaining butter in a large saucepan. Add the shallot and cook for 3–5 minutes until softened, then add the mussels and remaining cider. Cover the pan and cook for 5 minutes, or until the mussels have opened. Discard any that remain closed. Stir in the crème fraîche and parsley.

- Place the fish on serving plates and spoon over the mussels and sauce to serve.

Smoked Trout and Apple Cider Salad

Stir together 100 ml (3½ fl oz) mascarpone cheese, 1 tablespoon cider vinegar, 1–2 tablespoons horseradish sauce and a handful of dill, chopped. Break 2 x 100 g (3½ oz) skinless smoked trout fillets into large flakes, discarding any bones. Cut 2 apples into thin slices. Arrange on serving plates with 100 g (3½ oz) watercress, then drizzle over the dressing.

Baked Plaice with Cider Lentils

Heat 15 g (½ oz) butter and 1 tablespoon olive oil in a saucepan. Add 1 finely chopped shallot and cook for 3–5 minutes until softened. Add 2 thinly sliced back bacon rashers and 1 crushed garlic clove and cook for a further 2 minutes until lightly browned. Add 75 g (3 oz) rinsed and drained dried Puy lentils and pour over 200 ml (7 fl oz) cider.

Bring to the boil, then simmer for 15–20 minutes until just tender, topping up with water if necessary. Meanwhile, bake the plaice fillets as above. Spoon the lentils on to a plate and top with the plaice and a dollop of crème fraîche mixed with chopped flat leaf parsley.

QuickCook

Healthy

Recipes listed by cooking time

30

20

10

Steamed Sea Bream with Asian Flavours

Serves 2

1-cm (½-inch) piece of fresh root ginger
2 lemon grass stalks, finely chopped
1 garlic clove, sliced
½ red chilli, finely chopped
1 kaffir lime leaf, finely sliced
handful of coriander, chopped
3 tablespoons fish sauce
1 tablespoon vegetable oil, plus extra for oiling
2 sea bream fillets, about 150 g (5 oz) each
plain rice, to serve

- Peel the ginger and cut into matchsticks. Mix with the lemon grass, garlic, chilli, lime leaf, coriander, fish sauce and oil.

- Place each fish fillet on a lightly oiled piece of foil, skin-side down. Pour over the dressing. Fold the foil over tightly to seal, leaving a little air around the fish.

- Place the foil packets in a steamer set over simmering water. Cook for 10–15 minutes until the fish is just cooked through. Serve with plain rice.

Mussels with Asian Flavours

Heat 1 tablespoon vegetable oil in a large saucepan. Cook 2 finely chopped lemon grass stalks, 1-cm (½-inch) piece of fresh root ginger, peeled and cut into matchsticks, 1 sliced garlic clove and ½ finely chopped red chilli for 30 seconds. Add 3 tablespoons fish sauce, 50 ml (2 fl oz) coconut milk and 500 g (1 lb) cleaned live mussels. Cover and cook for about 5 minutes until the mussels have opened. Discard any that remain closed. Toss in 300 g (10 oz) straight-to-wok rice noodles, heat through and serve scattered with chopped coriander.

Fish Rice with Asian Flavours

Heat 2 teaspoons vegetable oil in a saucepan. Add 1 crushed garlic clove, ½ finely chopped green chilli and 1 teaspoon grated fresh root ginger and gently cook for 1 minute to soften. Add 1 finely chopped lemon grass stalk and 300 g (10 oz) brown long-grain rice. Pour over 600 ml (1 pint) water and season. Cover and simmer for 20 minutes, placing 2 x 150 g (5 oz) sea bream fillets on top of the rice for the last 5 minutes of cooking. Remove from the heat and leave to steam for about 8 minutes until the rice and fish are just cooked through. Scatter with chopped coriander and serve.

Tuna Burgers with Mango Salsa

Serves 4

1 large mango, stoned, peeled and sliced

¼ red onion, thinly sliced

2 tablespoons olive oil

juice of ½ lime

½ red chilli, finely chopped

handful of coriander, finely chopped

500 g (1 lb) piece of tuna, cut into large chunks

½ shallot, finely chopped

1 tablespoon soy sauce

4 ciabatta rolls, split

salt and pepper

- Toss together the mango, onion, 1 tablespoon of the oil, lime juice, chilli and coriander and set aside.

- Place the tuna in a food processor with the shallot and soy sauce. Briefly pulse until the mixture just comes together but isn't puréed. Lightly wet your hands, then shape into 4 burgers.

- Heat a griddle pan until smoking hot. Season the burgers and brush all over with the remaining oil. Cook the burgers on the pan for 1–2 minutes on each side, or until browned but still rare inside. Toast the ciabatta halves, then place a spoonful of mango salsa inside. Top with the burgers and serve.

Tuna Strips in Pitta Breads

Cut 500 g (1 lb) tuna into thin strips. Heat a griddle pan until smoking hot. Toss the tuna in a little olive oil. Cook on the pan on one side only for 1 minute. Toss with 1 tablespoon chopped red onion, ½ chopped mango and a handful of coriander leaves. Divide the mixture between 4 toasted pitta bread pockets, top each with a dollop of soured cream, if you like, and serve with lime wedges for squeezing over.

Tuna Steak Burgers with Teriyaki Onions

Rub a little olive oil over 4 x 150 g (5 oz) tuna steaks and place on a baking sheet. Place in a preheated oven, 110°C (225°F), Gas Mark ¼, for 20–25 minutes until cooked rare to medium. Meanwhile, heat 1 tablespoon olive oil in a frying pan. Add 1 sliced onion and cook over a low heat for 20 minutes until soft and caramelized. Add 2 tablespoons soy sauce, 1 tablespoon mirin and 2 teaspoons caster sugar.

Cook for a further 5 minutes until the liquid has evaporated. Place each tuna steak into a split burger bun and top with the onions.

20 Plaice with Beans and Chorizo

Serves 4

2 tablespoons olive oil

1 onion, finely chopped

2 garlic cloves, finely chopped

2 x 400 g (13 oz) cans flageolet
  beans, rinsed and drained

150 ml (¼ pint) vegetable stock

1 strip of orange rind

1 bay leaf

4 plaice fillets, about 150 g
  (5 oz) each

8 thin slices of chorizo

salt and pepper

handful of flat leaf parsley,
  chopped, to garnish

- Heat 1 tablespoon of the oil in a saucepan. Add the onion and garlic and cook for 5 minutes until softened. Add the beans, stock, orange rind and bay leaf and leave to simmer for 10 minutes until soft and most of the liquid has boiled away. Season well.

- Brush the remaining oil over the fish fillets. Cook under a preheated hot grill for 3–5 minutes on each side until the fish flakes easily. Meanwhile, place the chorizo in a dry, nonstick frying pan and cook for 1 minute on each side until brown and crisp.

- Remove the bay leaf and orange rind from the beans, then spoon on to serving plates, top with the fish and chorizo and scatter with the parsley.

---

10 Plaice with Chorizo and Bean Mash

Place 2 thin slices of chorizo on top of 4 x 150 g (5 oz) plaice fillets and cook under a preheated hot grill for 3–5 minutes on each side until the fish flakes easily. Meanwhile, place 2 rinsed and drained 400 g (13 oz) cans flageolet beans in a saucepan, pour over boiling water to cover and cook for 1 minute. Drain and mash together with 4 tablespoons milk. Serve alongside the fish.

30 Plaice with Chorizo Cassoulet

Heat 1 tablespoon olive oil in a saucepan. Add 1 finely chopped onion, 2 finely chopped garlic cloves and 50 g (2 oz) chopped chorizo and cook for 5 minutes. Add 2 rinsed and drained 400 g (13 oz) cans flageolet beans, 50 ml (2 fl oz) vegetable stock and 50 ml (2 fl oz) milk. Simmer for 5 minutes. Stir through 4 tablespoons half-fat crème fraîche and pour into a baking dish. Sprinkle over 50 g (2 oz) dried breadcrumbs mixed with the finely chopped leaves from 1 thyme sprig. Place in a preheated oven, 190°C (375°F), Gas Mark 5, for 10–15 minutes until bubbling and browned. Meanwhile, brush 1 tablespoon olive oil over 4 x 150 g (5 oz) plaice fillets. Cook under a preheated hot grill for 3–5 minutes on each side until the fish flakes easily. Serve the fish with the bean mixture.

3⦿ Healthy Fish Supper with Homemade Tomato Ketchup

Serves 4

750 g (1½ lb) potatoes, scrubbed and cut into chips

3 tablespoons olive oil

½ onion, sliced

1 teaspoon finely grated fresh root ginger

1 garlic clove, crushed

½ teaspoon ground coriander

1 tablespoon tomato purée

200 g (7 oz) cherry tomatoes

4 tablespoons white wine vinegar

2 tablespoons soft brown sugar

2 tablespoons low-fat mayonnaise

4 skinless cod loins, about 150 g (5 oz) each

75 g (3 oz) dried wholemeal breadcrumbs

finely grated rind of 1 lemon

salt and pepper

- Cook the chips in boiling water for 3 minutes until just starting to soften. Drain and pat dry with kitchen paper. Toss with 2 tablespoons of the oil, season with salt and pepper and place on a large baking tray. Place in a preheated oven, 220°C (425°F), Gas Mark 7, for 25 minutes until golden and cooked through.

- Meanwhile, heat the remaining oil in a saucepan. Add the onion and cook for 10 minutes until softened. Add the ginger, garlic, coriander and tomato purée and cook for a further 2 minutes. Add the tomatoes, vinegar, sugar and a splash of water. Leave to simmer for 10 minutes. Whizz in a small food processor or blender to form a chunky ketchup. Season and set aside.

- While the ketchup is simmering, spread the mayonnaise all over the cod loins. Toss together the breadcrumbs and lemon rind. Dip the fish in the breadcrumbs until coated all over. Place on a baking sheet and cook in the oven, with the chips, for 12 minutes until just cooked through. Serve with the chips and ketchup.

 Crunchy Tomato Fish Bites Cut 4 x 150 g (5 oz) skinless cod loins into bite-sized pieces. Toss with 2 tablespoons red pesto. Coat with 75 g (3 oz) dried wholemeal breadcrumbs. Drizzle with olive oil on a baking sheet. Place in a preheated oven, 220°C (425°F), Gas Mark 7, for 7 minutes until cooked. Serve with potato salad.

 Sea Bass with Tomato Pesto Pasta In a food processor, whizz together a large handful of basil, 1 crushed garlic clove, 25 g (1 oz) grated Parmesan cheese and 2 tablespoons olive oil. Cook 400 g (13 oz) dried linguine according to the packet instructions. Meanwhile, heat 2 teaspoons olive oil in a nonstick frying pan. Cut 2 x 150 g (5 oz) sea bass fillets into pieces and cook, skin-side down, for 3 minutes. Turn over and cook for 3 minutes more. Drain the pasta. Toss through the pesto and 100 g (3½ oz) halved cherry tomatoes, then the fish, first discarding the skin, if liked.

Sea Bream with Tomatoes and Basil

Serves 4

3 tablespoons olive oil

2 sea bream, about 500 g (1 lb) each, gutted and scaled

3 garlic cloves, sliced

150 g (5 oz) cherry tomatoes, halved

1 red chilli, sliced

50 ml (2 fl oz) dry white wine

200 ml (7 fl oz) water

handful of basil leaves, torn

salt and pepper

- Heat the oil in a large frying pan. Season the fish, then add to the pan with the garlic, tomatoes and chilli and cook for 1–2 minutes. Pour over the wine and the measurement water. Cook for 7 minutes. Carefully turn over the fish and cook for a further 7 minutes until just cooked. Transfer the fish to a warmed serving dish.

- Cook the sauce over a high heat for 30 seconds to reduce a little. Stir through the basil and pour over the fish. Serve 1 fillet per person with crusty bread and a green salad.

Thai-Style Fish with Tomatoes and Basil

Heat 1 tablespoon olive oil in a large, nonstick frying pan. Add 1 chopped garlic clove and 1 teaspoon finely chopped fresh root ginger. Cook for 30 seconds. Add 250 g (8 oz) skinless fish fillets, cut into chunks, and cook for 3 minutes. Add 100 g (3½ oz) cherry tomatoes and cook for 3 minutes. Mix together 1 tablespoon fish sauce and 1 teaspoon caster sugar and stir in. Cook for a further 1–2 minutes. Add a handful of chopped basil.

Baked Sea Bream with Tomatoes and Basil

Lightly oil 2 sheets of foil. Peel and slice 2 potatoes very thinly. Lay the slices in the centre of each piece of foil. Lay 2 small gutted and scaled sea bream on top of each. Divide 75 g (3 oz) chopped tomatoes between the fish cavities along with a handful of basil leaves. Scatter 75 g (3 oz) chopped tomatoes on top of the fish along with 2 teaspoons drained capers and a little olive oil. Season with salt and pepper.

Fold the foil over tightly to seal, leaving a little air around the fish, and place on a baking sheet. Place in a preheated oven, 220°C (425°F), Gas Mark 7, for 20–25 minutes until the fish and potatoes are cooked through. Serve 1 fillet per person.

30 Smoked Salmon Sushi Salad

Serves 4

250 g (8 oz) sushi rice, well rinsed
and very well drained
500 ml (17 fl oz) water
7 tablespoons rice vinegar
2 tablespoons caster sugar, plus
an extra pinch
2 tablespoons sesame seeds
3 tablespoons soy sauce
2 teaspoons finely grated fresh
root ginger
1 avocado, stoned, peeled and
sliced
200 g (7 oz) smoked salmon
slices
2 spring onions, sliced
2 tablespoons toasted, thinly
sliced nori sheets, to garnish
salt

- Place the rice in a saucepan, pour over the measurement water and season with salt. Bring to the boil, then cook for 10–12 minutes until most of the water has boiled away and small craters appear in the rice. Cover with a tight-fitting lid and leave to steam off the heat for 5 minutes. Meanwhile, mix together 4 tablespoons of the vinegar and the 2 tablespoons sugar until the sugar has dissolved.

- Tip the rice on to a baking sheet. Pour over the vinegar mixture and use a spatula to stir through in a slicing motion until the rice looks glossy. Cover with damp kitchen paper and leave to cool a little.

- Cook the sesame seeds in a small dry, frying pan over a low heat until lightly browned.

- Mix together the remaining vinegar, soy sauce, ginger and the pinch of sugar. Spoon the rice into serving bowls. Arrange the avocado, smoked salmon and spring onions on top. Drizzle over the dressing. Cut the toasted nori into thin strips and scatter over with the sesame seeds.

 Smoked Salmon Rice Crackers

Arrange 8 rice crackers on a serving plate. Top with 1 small chopped avocado and 100 g (3½ oz) smoked salmon strips. Drizzle over 1½ tablespoons each rice vinegar and soy sauce mixed with 1 teaspoon finely grated fresh root ginger and a pinch of sugar. Top with 1 sliced spring onion.

 Stir-Fried Salmon with Noodles

Heat 1 tablespoon vegetable oil in a nonstick wok or frying pan. Cut 2 x 125 g (4 oz) skinless salmon fillets into chunks, add to the pan and stir-fry for 5–7 minutes until just cooked. Remove. Add 1 sliced onion and stir-fry until softened. Add 1 crushed garlic clove and 1 teaspoon finely grated fresh root ginger and continue to stir-fry for 30 seconds. Toss in 300 g (10 oz) straight-to-wok rice noodles. Pour over 3 tablespoons soy sauce and 1 tablespoon mirin and cook for 1–2 minutes. Return the salmon to the pan with 100 g (3½ oz) watercress and cook until wilted.

20 Tomato and Fennel Fish Pie

Serves 4

4 tablespoons olive oil
1 fennel bulb, chopped
2 garlic cloves, sliced
200 g (7 oz) cherry tomatoes
1 tablespoon tomato purée
50 ml (2 fl oz) dry white wine
75 ml (3 fl oz) water

300 g (10 oz) skinless cod fillets,
    cut into chunks
150 g (5 oz) raw peeled large
    prawns
750 g (1½ lb) potatoes, peeled
    and cut into chunks
2 spring onions, sliced
salt and pepper

- Heat 1 tablespoon of the oil in a saucepan. Add the fennel and garlic and cook for 5–7 minutes until softened. Add the tomatoes and tomato purée and cook for a further 2 minutes until softened. Pour over the wine and cook until nearly boiled away, then add the measurement water and fish. Cook for 3 minutes. Add the prawns and cook for 3–5 minutes until just cooked through.

- Meanwhile, cook the potatoes in a saucepan of salted boiling water for 12–15 minutes until soft. Drain and mash with the remaining oil, the spring onions and a little water to loosen. Season well with salt and pepper.

- Arrange the fish and sauce in a baking dish. Spoon over the mash. Cook under a preheated hot grill for 3 minutes until browned. Serve immediately.

 Prawns with Tomato and Fennel Mayo Arrange 325 g (11 oz) cooked peeled large prawns on a plate. Mix together 3 tablespoons mayonnaise, 3 tablespoons fromage frais, 2 finely chopped sun-dried tomatoes, 1 teaspoon crushed fennel seeds and a squeeze of lemon juice. Serve with the prawns, a crisp green salad and some crusty brown bread.

 Cod with a Tomato, Fennel and Potato Crust Place 4 x 175 g (6 oz) cod fillets on a lightly oiled baking sheet. Season, then place 2 thinly sliced tomatoes on top. Sprinkle with 1 crushed garlic clove and ½ teaspoon coarsely ground fennel seeds. Use a mandolin or food processor to slice 2 peeled potatoes very thinly. Arrange the potato slices on top of the tomatoes and lightly brush with olive oil. Place in a preheated oven, 190 °C (375 °F), Gas Mark 5, for 20 minutes until the fish is cooked through and the potatoes are crisp.

Halibut Ceviche with Grapefruit and Chillies

Serves 2

450 g (14½ oz) skinless halibut fillet

2 limes

1 grapefruit

100 g (3½ oz) cherry tomatoes, halved

1 red chilli, deseeded (optional) and sliced

handful of mint, finely chopped

1 tablespoon extra virgin olive oil

salt and pepper

- Using a very sharp knife, cut the fish into thin slices.

- Grate the rind from 1 lime into a medium-sized bowl, then squeeze in the juice from both limes. Cut off the base of the grapefruit, then cut around the flesh to remove the rind and pith. Slice into segments and set aside. Add any juice from the grapefruit to the bowl. Add the fish to the lime and grapefruit juices and toss to coat. Leave to marinate for 15 minutes.

- Discard the marinade from the fish. Arrange the fish on a serving plate with the grapefruit segments and tomatoes. Scatter over the chilli and mint, season and drizzle with the oil to serve.

 Spicy Halibut and Grapefruit Salad

Mix together 1 tablespoon vegetable oil, ½ finely chopped red chilli and a handful of coriander, finely chopped. Toss with 450 g (14½ oz) skinless halibut fillet, cut into bite-sized pieces. Cook under a preheated hot grill for 2–3 minutes on each side. Meanwhile, peel 3 segments of grapefruit and cut into small pieces. Whisk together 1 tablespoon vegetable oil and 1 tablespoon rice vinegar. Toss with 100 g (3½ oz) mixed salad leaves and another handful of coriander leaves, top with the grapefruit and halibut and serve.

 Halibut with Grapefruit Quinoa Salad Place 325 g (11 oz) quinoa in a saucepan. Pour over 500 ml (17 fl oz) water and season with salt. Bring to the boil, then cover with a tight-fitting lid and simmer for 15 minutes. Cool for 1 minute. Meanwhile, rub a little olive oil over 1 red pepper. Cook under a preheated hot grill for about 10 minutes until blackened all over. Seal in a freezer bag for 5 minutes. Working over a bowl to catch the juices, cut off the base of a grapefruit, then cut around to remove the rind. Slice 1 half into segments and squeeze the juice from the other half. Mix the grapefruit juice with ½ teaspoon grated fresh root ginger, 1 teaspoon clear honey and 1 tablespoon olive oil. Toss through the quinoa. Peel away the skin of the pepper, discard the core and seeds and chop. Add to the quinoa with 2 sliced spring onions, the grapefruit segments and a handful of coriander leaves. Rub a little vegetable oil over 450 g (14½ oz) skinless halibut fillet and cook under the grill for 4–5 minutes on each side until cooked through. Serve with the salad.

Oven-Baked Thai Fishcakes

Serves 4

500 g (1 lb) skinless firm white fish fillets
2 tablespoons fish sauce
1 tablespoon Thai red curry paste
1 teaspoon caster sugar
75 g (3 oz) green beans, thinly sliced
handful of coriander, chopped
2 teaspoons vegetable oil
salt and pepper

To serve

sweet chilli sauce
cucumber wedges

- Place the fish, fish sauce, curry paste and sugar in a food processor and whizz until smooth. Stir through the green beans and coriander, then season.

- Brush a 12-hole muffin tray with the oil, then spoon 2–3 tablespoons of the mixture inside each hole. Lightly press down. Place in a preheated oven, 200°C (400°F), Gas Mark 6, for 12–15 minutes until golden and cooked through. Serve with sweet chilli sauce and cucumber wedges.

Thai Fish Salad
Cut 300 g (10 oz) skinless firm white fish fillets into large chunks. Cover with boiling water and simmer for 3–5 minutes until cooked through. Drain. Mix together 1 chopped red chilli, 2 tablespoons fish sauce, 1 tablespoon caster sugar and the juice of 1 lime. Toss with 75 g (3 oz) cooked peeled large prawns and the fish. Add 200 g (7 oz) crisp salad leaves and toss again. Sprinkle over 25 g (1 oz) chopped roasted peanuts.

Thai Salmon Cakes with Dipping Sauce
In a food processor, whizz together 500 g (1 lb) skinless salmon fillet, 1 egg white, 2 tablespoons fish sauce, 1 tablespoon Thai green curry paste and 1 tablespoon caster sugar until smooth. Mix in 1 finely chopped kaffir lime leaf and a handful of coriander, chopped. Shape into 12 patties. Chill for 5–10 minutes to firm up. Heat 2 tablespoons vegetable oil in a frying pan. Cook the fishcakes for 5–7 minutes on each side until golden and cooked through. Meanwhile, make a dipping sauce by heating 3 tablespoons white wine vinegar, 2 tablespoons caster sugar and 50 ml (2 fl oz) water in a saucepan until the sugar has dissolved. Keep cooking until it turns syrupy. Leave to cool. Stir through 1 tablespoon finely chopped cucumber, 1 chopped red chilli and 2 teaspoons fish sauce. Serve with the fishcakes.

30 Cod in Tomato and Olive Sauce

Serves 4

1 tablespoon olive oil
1 onion, sliced
2 garlic cloves, finely chopped
1 tablespoon tomato purée
400 g (13 oz) can chopped
   tomatoes
pinch of sugar
handful of thyme leaves
4 skinless cod fillets, about 125 g
   (4 oz) each
25 g (1 oz) pitted black olives
salt and pepper
new potatoes, to serve (optional)

- Heat the oil in a large, deep frying pan. Add the onion and cook for 5 minutes until softened, then add the garlic and cook for a further 2 minutes. Stir in the tomato purée and cook for 1 minute, then pour over the tomatoes. Add the sugar and thyme and season, then reduce the heat and leave to simmer for 10 minutes.

- Slide the fish fillets into the sauce along with the olives, cover loosely with kitchen foil and leave to simmer for 8–10 minutes until the fish flakes easily. Serve with some boiled new potatoes, if you like.

 Cod with Tapenade and Tomatoes

Spread 4 teaspoons tapenade over 4 x 125 g (4 oz) thin cod fillets. Thinly slice 1 tomato and place 1 slice on top of each piece of fish. Drizzle with a little olive oil. Cook under a preheated hot grill for 7–10 minutes until the fish is just cooked through.

 Olive-Crusted Cod with Tomato Salad

Finely chop 25 g (1 oz) pitted olives and mix with 50 g (2 oz) dried breadcrumbs and a handful of chopped flat leaf parsley. Rub 1 tablespoon olive oil over 4 x 200 g (7 oz) cod fillets, place on a baking sheet and press the breadcrumb mixture on top. Place in a preheated oven, 200°C (400°F), Gas Mark 6, for 15 minutes until the fish is cooked through. Five minutes before the end of cooking, whisk together 1 tablespoon olive oil, 1 teaspoon white wine vinegar and a pinch of sugar. Toss with 200 g (7 oz) cherry tomatoes and a large handful of basil leaves. Serve with the fish.

Smoked Trout, Cucumber and Radish Salad

Serves 2

2 tablespoons mayonnaise

2 tablespoons fromage frais

lemon juice, to taste

125 g (4 oz) skinless smoked trout fillets, broken into large flakes

½ cucumber, sliced

6 radishes, thinly sliced

50 g (2 oz) watercress

pepper

toasted country-style bread, to serve

- Mix together the mayonnaise and fromage frais with lemon juice to taste and season well with pepper.

- Arrange the trout, cucumber, radishes and watercress on a serving plates. Drizzle over the mayonnaise mixture and serve with plenty of toasted country-style bread.

 Trout with Radish and Cucumber Tzatziki Rub olive oil over 2 x 125 g (4 oz) trout, gutted and scaled, and season. Place a lemon slice in each fish cavity, then cook on a hot barbecue or under a preheated hot grill for 7 minutes on each side, or until the fish flakes easily. Meanwhile, finely chop ¼ cucumber and thinly slice 3 radishes. Mix with 1 small crushed garlic clove, 75 g (3 oz) natural yogurt and some finely chopped dill. Serve alongside the trout.

 Trout, Pickled Cucumber and Radish Salad Thinly slice ½ cucumber and mix with 1 tablespoon each caster sugar and rice vinegar and a pinch of salt. Leave to stand for 25 minutes until lightly pickled. Drain and toss together with 6 thinly sliced radishes and a handful of flat leaf parsley, chopped. Serve the salad with 125 g (4 oz) smoked trout fillets, kept whole, and some steamed new potatoes.

30 Coconut Fish Curry

Serves 4

1 tablespoon vegetable oil
½ teaspoon mustard seeds
1 teaspoon cumin seeds
10 curry leaves
1 onion, chopped
1 tablespoon finely chopped fresh
  root ginger
1 garlic clove, finely chopped
1 red chilli, finely chopped
1 teaspoon ground coriander
½ teaspoon turmeric
200 ml (7 fl oz) water
1 tablespoon tamarind purée
4 halibut steaks, about 175 g
  (6 oz) each
3 tomatoes, chopped
100 ml (3½ fl oz) half-fat
  coconut milk
salt and pepper
plain boiled rice, to serve

- Heat the oil in a large frying pan over a high heat. Add the seeds and cook for a few seconds until they start to pop, then add the curry leaves and cook for another few seconds until they turn golden. Reduce the heat, add the onion, ginger, garlic and chilli and cook over a medium heat for 5 minutes until softened.

- Add the coriander and turmeric and cook for 30 seconds. Stir in the measurement water and tamarind and leave to simmer for 5 minutes. Add the fish and tomatoes, cover and gently cook for about 5 minutes, or until the fish is just cooked through. Pour over the coconut milk and heat through. Season and serve with plain boled rice.

---

1 Curried Coconut Fish Fingers

Cut 4 x 175 g (6 oz) halibut steaks into long, thin slices. Rub 1 tablespoon curry paste over the fish slices, then press into 50 g (2 oz) desiccated coconut until coated. Drizzle with a little vegetable oil. Cook under a hot grill for 3 minutes. Turn over and cook for a further 3 minutes until just cooked through.

2 Griddled Fish with Coconut Rice

Place 300 g (10 oz) white long-grain rice in a saucepan. Pour over 200 ml (7 fl oz) coconut milk and 400 ml (14 fl oz) water and season with salt. Bring to the boil, then cover and simmer for 15 minutes until the rice is just tender. Meanwhile, mix together ½ finely chopped red chilli, a handful of coriander leaves, chopped, and 2 teaspoons vegetable oil. Toss with 4 x 175 g (6 oz) halibut steaks and season. Heat a griddle pan until smoking hot. Cook the fish for 5 minutes on each side until just cooked through. Serve alongside the rice.

Grilled Sea Bass with Salsa Verde

Serves 4

olive oil, for oiling

4 sea bass fillets, about 150 g
(5 oz) each

salt and pepper

For the salsa verde

3 tablespoons olive oil

large handful of flat leaf parsley

small handful of basil

1 garlic clove, crushed

juice of ½ lemon

1 tablespoon drained capers

To serve

boiled new potatoes

green salad

- Rub a little olive oil over the fish fillets and season. Heat a griddle pan until smoking hot. Griddle the fish fillets skin-side down for 7 minutes until the skin is crisp and golden. Turn over and cook for a further 5 minutes until just cooked through.

- Meanwhile, whizz together the salsa verde ingredients in a small food processor until you have a rough paste.

- Place the fish on serving plates and spoon over the salsa verde. Serve with boiled new potatoes and a green salad.

Spaghetti with Salsa Verde and Tuna

Prepare the salsa verde as above, then stir in 150 g (5 oz) drained canned tuna. Meanwhile, cook 500 g (1 lb) fresh spaghetti according to the packet instructions. Drain the pasta, return to the pan and toss through the tuna and salsa verde. Serve immediately.

Sea Bass Stuffed with Salsa Verde

Prepare the salsa verde as above. Divide 2 sea bass, about 1.25 kg (2½ lb) each, gutted and scaled, into fillets and season. Thinly slice 1 lemon and lay half the slices down a lightly oiled baking sheet. Cover with 2 fish fillets, skin-side down. Spread the salsa verde all over the fish, then lay the other fillets on top. Cover with the remaining lemon slices. Cook in a preheated oven, 230°C (450°F), Gas Mark 8, for 15–20 minutes until just cooked through. Place on a warm serving platter and serve with boiled new potatoes and a green salad.

Oatmeal Herrings with Beetroot Salad

Serves 4

50 g (2 oz) plain flour
1 egg, beaten
100 g (3½ oz) medium or coarse oatmeal
4 boned and butterflied herrings, about 175 g (6 oz) each
3 tablespoons vegetable oil
½ shallot, finely chopped
1 tablespoon sherry vinegar
3 tablespoons extra virgin olive oil
175 g (6 oz) ready-cooked fresh beetroot, thinly sliced
100 g (3½ oz) watercress
1 orange, peeled and segmented
salt and pepper

- Place the flour, egg and oatmeal on separate plates. Season the herrings, then dip into the flour until coated all over. Place the flesh side only into the egg. Leave any excess egg to drip off, then press into the oatmeal until coated.

- Heat the oil in a large, nonstick frying pan. Cook the herrings, oatmeal-side down, for 3–5 minutes until browned. Turn over and cook for a further 3 minutes until the skin is crisp.

- Whisk together the shallot, vinegar and oil, then season well. Toss with the beetroot, watercress and orange. Arrange on serving plates with the herrings.

 Kipper Salad with Oatmeal Topping
Cook 25 g (1 oz) oatmeal gently in a dry frying pan for 3–5 minutes until golden. Season and cool. Whisk together ½ finely chopped shallot, 1 tablespoon sherry vinegar and 3 tablespoons extra virgin olive oil. Season well. Toss with 200 g (7 oz) skinless kipper fillets, torn into chunks, 175 g (6 oz) thinly sliced ready-cooked fresh beetroot, 100 g (3½ oz) watercress and 1 peeled and segmented orange. Sprinkle with the oatmeal, then serve.

 Oatmeal Kipper Cakes with Beetroot Salad Cook 2 peeled and chopped potatoes in a saucepan of lightly salted boiling water for 12–15 minutes until soft. Drain, then roughly mash and mix with 300 g (10 oz) skinless kipper fillets. Use your hands to form into 4–6 large fishcakes. Place 50 g (2 oz) plain flour, 1 beaten egg and 100 g (3½ oz) medium or coarse oatmeal on separate plates. Dip the fishcakes into the flour, then into the egg and finally press into the oatmeal until coated. Heat 3 tablespoons vegetable oil in a large, nonstick frying pan. Cook the fishcakes for 3–5 minutes on each side, or until golden all over. Meanwhile, prepare the beetroot salad as above. Serve the fishcakes with the salad.

Roasted Salmon with Peach Salsa

Serves 4

1½ tablespoons olive oil
4 salmon steaks, about 150 g
  (5 oz) each
2 peaches, stoned and chopped
½ teaspoon finely grated fresh
  root ginger
juice of ½ lime
1 tablespoon finely chopped red
  onion
½ green chilli, sliced
handful of basil, chopped
salt and pepper

- Rub ½ teaspoon of the oil over the salmon steaks and season well. Cook under a preheated hot grill for 5 minutes. Turn over and cook for a further 3–5 minutes until just cooked through.

- Meanwhile, mix the remaining oil with the remaining ingredients. Spoon over the salmon to serve.

2 Barbecued Salmon with Peach Sauce

Roughly chop 2 peaches. Place in a saucepan with 5 tablespoons tomato ketchup, 1 tablespoon cider vinegar, 1 tablespoon soft brown sugar, a squeeze of lime juice and a pinch of chilli flakes. Simmer for 10 minutes. Whizz in a food processor until smooth. Lightly oil 4 x 150 g (5 oz) salmon fillets and brush all over with the sauce. Cook on a hot barbecue, skin-side down, for 5 minutes. Turn over, brush with any remaining sauce and cook for a further 3 minutes until cooked through, then serve.

3 Peach and Ginger Baked Salmon

In a food processor, roughly whizz together 2 stoned peaches, 1 teaspoon finely chopped fresh root ginger, 1 tablespoon rice vinegar and a handful of basil leaves until you have a chunky sauce. Place 1 x 625 g (1¼ lb) whole salmon fillet on a lightly oiled baking sheet. Pour over the peach sauce, season and drizzle with olive oil. Place in preheated oven, 200°C (400°F), Gas Mark 6, for 20 minutes, or until just cooked through.

30 Couscous and White Fish Parcels

Serves 4

300 ml (½ pint) hot vegetable
  stock
75 g (3 oz) frozen broad beans
75 g (3 oz) frozen peas
200 g (7 oz) couscous
2 spring onions, sliced
4 sea bass fillets, about 150 g
  (5 oz) each, skin on
1 lemon, sliced
1 tablespoon extra virgin olive oil
50 ml (2 fl oz) natural yogurt
handful of dill, chopped
salt and pepper

- Bring the stock to the boil in a saucepan, add the beans and cook for 1 minute. Add the peas and cook for a further 2 minutes. Pour the stock and vegetables over the couscous in a heatproof bowl. Cover with clingfilm and leave to stand for 7–10 minutes until the couscous has swelled. Stir through the spring onions with a fork.

- Divide the couscous between 4 large sheets of nonstick baking paper set on a large baking sheet. Place a fish fillet on top of each, then top with lemon slices, drizzle with the oil and season. Fold the paper over tightly to seal, leaving a little air around the fish.

- Place in a preheated oven, 200°C (400°F), Gas Mark 6, for 15 minutes until the parcels puff a little. Meanwhile, mix together the yogurt and dill. Open the parcels at the table and spoon over the yogurt.

10 One-Pot Couscous

Cook 150 g (5 oz) frozen peas in 300 ml (½ pint) boiling vegetable stock for 2 minutes. Meanwhile, heat 1 tablespoon olive oil in a large frying pan. Add 4 x 150 g (5 oz) skinless sea bass fillets, cut into chunks, and fry for 1 minute. Add 2 sliced garlic cloves and cook for a further 1 minute. Stir in 200 g (7 oz) couscous and the stock and peas. Cover and leave to stand for 7 minutes. Stir through 1 sliced spring onion and some chopped dill. Drizzle with natural yogurt and serve.

20 Couscous Bites with Mushed Peas

Place 200 g (7 oz) couscous in a heatproof bowl. Pour over 300 ml (½ pint) hot vegetable stock, cover with clingfilm and leave to stand for 7 minutes to swell. Stir in a handful of dill, chopped. Cut 4 x 150 g (5 oz) skinless sea bass fillets into chunks. Dust 2 tablespoons plain flour over the fish, then dip in 1 beaten egg. Add to the couscous and coat all over. Heat 1 tablespoon olive oil in a nonstick pan and cook the fish for 3–4 minutes on each side. Meanwhile, cook 200 g (7 oz) frozen peas in a saucepan of lightly salted boiling water for 3 minutes until tender. Drain and whizz in a food processor with 1 chopped spring onion and 2 tablespoons natural yogurt. Serve alongside the fish.

20 Asian Fishball Soup

Serves 4

1.5 litres (2½ pints) light fish or chicken stock

1.5-cm (¾-inch) piece of fresh root ginger, peeled

2 garlic cloves, peeled

1 red chilli, halved

4 tablespoons Shaoxing wine or dry sherry

300 g (10 oz) skinless haddock fillet, cubed

1 egg white

4 tablespoons rice flour

1 tablespoon soy sauce

2 pak choi, sliced

150 g (5 oz) dried medium egg noodles

150 g (5 oz) canned bamboo shoots, drained

2 spring onions, sliced

- Heat the stock in a large saucepan. Add the ginger, garlic, 1 chilli half and the Shaoxing wine or sherry and simmer while you make the fishballs.

- Place the fish, egg white, rice flour and soy sauce in a food processor and whizz until really smooth. Lightly wet your hands, then shape into walnut-sized balls.

- Remove the ginger, garlic and chilli from the stock. Add the fishballs and cook for 3 minutes.

- Add the pak choi to the stock and simmer for 5 minutes. Meanwhile, cook the noodles according to the pack instructions. Drain, then stir into the soup along with the bamboo shoots and heat through.

- Ladle into serving bowls and top with the remaining chilli, finely chopped, and the spring onions.

---

10 Stir-Fried Fish with Greens

Heat 1 tablespoon vegetable oil in a wok or large frying pan. Cut 300 g (10 oz) skinless white fish fillet into large pieces. Dust with a little cornflour. Cook, stirring often, for 1–2 minutes. Add 2 sliced pak choi and 100 g (3½ oz) halved shiitake mushrooms. Cook for a further 3 minutes until the fish is cooked through. Stir in 2 tablespoons each soy sauce and rice wine and heat through. Serve with rice noodles.

30 Asian Fishballs in Fresh Broth

Heat 1 tablespoon vegetable oil in a saucepan. Add 1 chopped shallot and cook for 2 minutes until softened. Add 2 peeled garlic cloves, a 1.5-cm (¾-inch) piece of fresh root ginger, peeled, and the bones from 3 fish. Cook for a further 3 minutes. Pour over 2 litres (3½ pints) light fish or chicken stock and leave to simmer for 15 minutes. Meanwhile, make the fishballs as above. Strain the stock into a clean saucepan. Add the fishballs and cook for 3 minutes. Add 2 sliced pak choi and simmer for 3 minutes, then stir in 150 g (5 oz) straight-to-wok rice noodles and 150 g (5 oz) drained canned bamboo shoots and cook for a further 2 minutes until the pak choi is tender and the noodles and bamboo shoots are heated through, then serve.

10 Prawn and Fennel Salad with Basil Citrus Dressing

Serves 2

½ orange
½ lime
½ small shallot, chopped
25 g (1 oz) basil leaves
4 tablespoons extra virgin olive oil
1 fennel bulb, thinly sliced
100 g (3½ oz) bag mixed salad leaves
150 g (5 oz) cooked peeled large prawns
salt and pepper

- Squeeze the juice of the orange and lime into a small food processor, add the shallot and basil and pulse briefly. With the motor running, slowly add the oil in a thin stream to make a smooth dressing, then season.

- Arrange the remaining ingredients on serving plates. Drizzle over the dressing and serve.

 20 Prawns, Mussels and Fennel with Basil Sauce Heat 1 tablespoon olive oil in a saucepan. Add 1 each finely chopped shallot and fennel bulb and cook for 5 minutes until softened. Add 1 crushed garlic clove and 3 skinned, deseeded and chopped tomatoes. Cook for 2–3 minutes. Add 100 ml (3½ fl oz) water, 75 g (3 oz) raw peeled large prawns and 200 g (7 oz) cleaned live mussels. Cover and cook for about 5 minutes until the mussels have opened and the prawns are cooked through. Discard any mussels that remain closed. Whizz together a large handful of basil, 4 tablespoons olive oil and a squeeze of lemon juice in a small food processor. Drizzle over the seafood.

 30 Creamy Fennel and Prawn Risotto Heat 2 tablespoons olive oil in a deep frying pan. Add 1 finely chopped onion and 1 chopped fennel bulb and cook for 5 minutes until softened. Stir in 150 g (5 oz) risotto rice until well coated. Finely grate over the rind of ½ lemon. Pour in 75 ml (3 fl oz) dry vermouth and cook until nearly boiled away. Add about 325 ml (11 fl oz) hot vegetable stock, a ladleful at a time, stirring and simmering after each addition until the stock is absorbed before adding the next. Continue until all the stock is absorbed and the rice is tender, about 15 minutes. Stir through 100 g (3½ oz) cooked peeled large prawns and leave to stand for 2 minutes before serving.

30 Spiced Fish Tagine

Serves 4

3 garlic cloves, peeled
1 teaspoon ground cumin
1 teaspoon ground paprika
pinch of turmeric
juice of 1 lemon
large handful of coriander,
    chopped
handful of flat leaf parsley,
    chopped
2 tablespoons olive oil
2 halibut steaks, about 225 g
    (7½ oz) each
200 g (7 oz) new potatoes,
    halved
1 green pepper, sliced
200 g (7 oz) cherry tomatoes,
    halved
75 g (3 oz) pitted black olives
100 ml (3½ fl oz) water
salt and pepper

- Use a pestle and mortar to crush 2 of the garlic cloves and pound together with the spices, lemon juice, most of the coriander, the parsley and 1 tablespoon of the oil until you have a paste. Alternatively, use a small food processor. Rub most of the paste all over the halibut steaks, season and leave to marinate.

- Cook the potatoes in a saucepan of lightly salted boiling water for 10 minutes, then drain. Meanwhile, heat a saucepan, add the remaining oil and garlic clove, sliced, and cook for a couple of seconds. Add the green pepper and cook for 2 minutes. Stir in the tomatoes, olives and remaining spice paste and cook until the tomatoes start to soften.

- Place the potatoes in a tagine or deep frying pan with a lid. Scatter over half the tomato mixture, then add the fish. Spoon the remaining tomato mixture on top, then drizzle over the measurement water. Cover and cook for 10–15 minutes until the fish is cooked through. Serve with couscous or crusty bread.

---

10 Spiced Fish Pittas
Pound together
2 crushed garlic cloves,
1 teaspoon each ground cumin
and paprika, the juice of 1 lemon,
a handful each of coriander and
parsley, chopped, and 1 tablespoon
olive oil. Smear over 4 x 150 g
(5 oz) tilapia fillets. Cook under a
preheated hot grill for 2½ minutes
each side. Serve in toasted pitta
bread with salad leaves.

20 One-Pot Spiced Fish Couscous
Cook 1 thinly sliced onion,
1 chopped garlic clove and
2 teaspoons finely chopped fresh
root ginger in 1 tablespoon olive
oil in a deep frying pan for about
5 minutes until soft and starting
to brown. Meanwhile, make the
spice paste (see left). Stir around
the pan. Add 4 x 175 g (6 oz)
halibut steaks. Cook for 2 minutes

on each side. Stir in 375 g (12 oz)
couscous and 150 g (5 oz) halved
cherry tomatoes. Pour over 400
ml (14 fl oz) hot vegetable stock.
Stir once. Cover and leave to
stand for 5–8 minutes until the
fish is cooked through. Stir in
2 tablespoons extra virgin olive
oil and a handful of coriander,
chopped before serving.

Grilled Mackerel with Lemon, Chilli and Coriander

Serves 4

grated rind and juice of 1 lemon
1 green chilli, finely chopped
handful of coriander, chopped,
   plus extra to garnish
1 tablespoon vegetable oil, plus
   extra for oiling
4 medium mackerel, scaled and
   gutted
salt and pepper

- Mix together the lemon rind and juice, chilli, coriander and oil. Using a sharp knife, make 3 shallow slashes across either side of each fish. Season and rub all over with the lemon mixture.

- Place the fish in a lightly oiled grill pan and cook under a preheated hot grill for about 7 minutes. Turn over and cook for a further 5 minutes, or until the fish is just cooked through. Scatter over chopped coriander and serve with lemon wedges, chapatis and a tomato salad.

 Spiced Smoked Mackerel Pâté

Mash 2 x 150 g (5 oz) skinless smoked mackerel fillets with a fork or in a food processor. Stir through 5 tablespoons low-fat cream cheese, then add a squeeze of lemon juice, ½ finely chopped green chilli and a handful of coriander, chopped. Serve with naan bread and a green salad.

 Mackerel in a Rich Curry Sauce

Heat 1 tablespoon vegetable oil in a saucepan. Add 1 thinly sliced onion and cook for about 8 minutes until soft and golden. Stir in 2 chopped garlic cloves and 2 teaspoons finely chopped fresh root ginger. Cook for 30 seconds, then add 2 teaspoons each ground cumin and coriander and ½ teaspoon turmeric. Pour over 2 x 400 g (13 oz) cans chopped tomatoes and simmer for 10 minutes. Meanwhile, cut 100 g (3½ oz) skin-on mackerel fillets into large chunks. Add to the curry along with a large handful of coriander, chopped. Simmer for 7–10 minutes until the fish is cooked through. Serve with plain basmati rice or naan bread.

QuickCook
Entertaining

Recipes listed by cooking time

3

2

3⚪ Bouillabaisse

Serves 4

4 tablespoons olive oil
1 onion, chopped
1 celery stick, chopped
1 large fennel bulb, sliced
5 garlic cloves, crushed
½ teaspoon ground coriander
½ teaspoon cayenne
400 g (13 oz) can chopped
   tomatoes
1 bouquet garni
pinch of saffron threads
2 litres (3½ pints) fish stock
2 kg (4 lb) non-oily fish fillets and
   shellfish of your choice
6 tablespoons mayonnaise
1 ready-roasted red pepper
salt and pepper
slices of lightly toasted baguette,
   to serve

- Heat the oil in a large saucepan. Add the onion, celery, fennel and 4 of the garlic cloves and gently cook for 7 minutes until softened. Stir in the ground coriander and cayenne and cook for a couple of seconds, then add the tomatoes, bouquet garni, saffron and stock and bring to the boil. Season, reduce the heat and leave to simmer for 10 minutes.

- Add any firmer-fleshed fish first, such as monkfish and langoustines, and cook for 5 minutes. Add any remaining fish or shellfish and simmer for a further 5 minutes until cooked through. Discard any shellfish that remains closed.

- Whizz together the remaining crushed garlic clove with the mayonnaise and red pepper. Drizzle on the baguette and serve alongside the stew.

 Garlicky Prawn Couscous

Cook 1 sliced garlic clove in a little olive oil for 2 minutes. Add 325 g (11 oz) couscous, 375 ml (13 fl oz) hot vegetable stock with a pinch of saffron and 200 g (7 oz) cooked peeled prawns. Cover and stand for 5–7 minutes, then fork through 100 g (3½ oz) sliced cherry tomatoes and some chopped parsley. Mix together the garlic, mayonnaise and red pepper as above and drizzle over to serve.

 Clam Soup with Garlicky Mayonnaise

Heat 2 tablespoons olive oil in a saucepan. Add 1 finely chopped onion and cook for 5 minutes until softened. Pour over 1 litre (1¾ pints) water, a 200 g (7 oz) can chopped tomatoes and a pinch of saffron threads. Leave to simmer for 7 minutes. Add 150 g (5 oz) soup pasta along with 500 g (1 lb) cleaned live clams and simmer, covered, for about 5 minutes until the clams have opened and the pasta is cooked through. Discard any clams that remain closed. Meanwhile, in a food processor, whizz together 6 tablespoons mayonnaise, 1 ready-roasted red pepper from a jar and 1 crushed garlic clove. Drizzle over the soup to serve.

30 Crispy Rice Paper Salmon Parcels with Soy Dressing

Serves 4

3 tablespoons rice vinegar

3 tablespoons soy sauce

1 tablespoon rice wine

1 tablespoon caster sugar

4 large rice paper wrappers

4 thin skinless salmon fillets,
about 75 g (3 oz) each

4 coriander sprigs

1 tablespoon vegetable oil

2 spring onions, sliced

salt and pepper

To serve

steamed rice

cooked edamame (soya) beans

- Mix together the vinegar, soy sauce, rice wine and sugar. Dip each rice paper wrapper into a bowl of very hot water for 30 seconds, or until softened. Brush a little of the soy mixture over each salmon fillet. Arrange a coriander sprig in the centre of each wrapper, then place a salmon fillet on top, presentation-side down. Fold over the edges of the wrapper to make a parcel. Repeat with the remaining salmon fillets.

- Heat the vegetable oil in a large, nonstick frying pan. Brush over the parcels with a little water, then cook for 4 minutes on each side until golden and crisp and the fish is cooked through.

- Stir the spring onion through the remaining soy dressing. Spoon over the fish and serve with steamed rice and edamame (soya) beans.

---

1 Salmon and Coriander Parcels

Cut 4 x 75 g (3 oz) thin skinless salmon fillets into thick strips. Dip the same number of small rice paper wrappers as salmon strips into a bowl of very hot water for 30 seconds, or until softened. Place on damp kitchen paper. Place a coriander sprig and salmon strip in the centre of each wrapper and roll up. Heat 4 tablespoons vegetable oil in a large frying pan. Cook the parcels for 2–3 minutes, turning occasionally, until golden and crisp all over. Serve with soy sauce for dipping.

2 Salmon Teriyaki Spring Rolls

Brush 5 tablespoons teriyaki sauce all over 2 x 175 g (6 oz) salmon fillets and drizzle with a little vegetable oil. Cook under a hot grill for 3–5 minutes on each side. Leave to cool a little, then discard the skin and break into flakes. Mix together with 1 finely grated carrot, 1 finely chopped spring onion and 50 g (2 oz) bean sprouts. Place heaped spoonfuls on spring roll wrappers, then fold over and roll up like a cigar. Mix together 1 tablespoon each cornflour and water. Brush along the ends of the wrappers to secure. Fill a large, deep saucepan one-third full with vegetable oil and heat until a cube of bread browns in 30 seconds. Deep-fry the spring rolls in batches for 3–5 minutes until golden. Drain on kitchen paper. Serve with more teriyaki sauce for dipping.

Lemon Sole with Pea Purée and Prosciutto

Serves 4

15 g (½ oz) butter
2 tablespoons olive oil
2 shallots, finely chopped
1 potato, peeled and diced
100 ml (3½ fl oz) fresh fish stock
leaves from 1 thyme sprig
1 bay leaf
2 tablespoons single cream
300 g (10 oz) frozen peas
4 slices of prosciutto
4 lemon sole fillets, about
    175 g (6 oz) each
plain flour, for dusting
lemon juice, to taste
salt and pepper

- Heat the butter and 1 tablespoon of the oil in a saucepan. Add the shallots and cook for 5 minutes until softened. Add the potato, stock and herbs and simmer for 10 minutes until the potato is just cooked through. Remove the herbs and add the cream and peas. Cook for 3 minutes until just tender.

- Meanwhile, heat the remaining oil in a large, nonstick frying pan. Add the prosciutto and cook for 1–2 minutes on each side until golden. Drain on kitchen paper. Season the sole fillets, dust with flour and cook for 3–5 minutes on each side until just cooked through.

- Scoop out a handful of peas from the pan and reserve. Whizz the remaining contents in a food processor until really smooth, then return with the whole peas to the pan. Season well and add lemon juice to taste. Spoon on to serving places, then top with the fish and prosciutto to serve.

 Pea Shoot, Parma Ham and Prawn Salad Heat 1 teaspoon olive oil in a nonstick frying pan. Add 3 slices of Parma ham and cook for 1–2 minutes on each side until crisp. Gently toss together 150 g (5 oz) cooked peeled small prawns, 100 g (3½ oz) pea shoots, 3 tablespoons olive oil and a good squeeze of lemon juice. Crumble over the Parma ham and serve.

 Lemon Sole with Pea and Leek Risotto Heat 25 g (1 oz) butter and 1 tablespoon vegetable oil in a deep frying pan. Add 1 sliced large leek and a splash of water. Cook for about 5 minutes until soft. Stir in 375 g (12 oz) risotto rice until well coated. Pour in 100 ml (3½ fl oz) dry white wine and boil until reduced. Add 900 ml (1½ pints) hot vegetable stock, a ladleful at a time, stirring and simmering after each addition until the stock is absorbed before adding the next. After about 15 minutes when all the stock is absorbed and the rice is nearly cooked, add 150 g (5 oz) frozen peas. Cook for a further 5 minutes. Meanwhile, heat 1 tablespoon olive oil in a large, nonstick frying pan. Season 4 x 175 g (6 oz) lemon sole fillets, dust with flour and cook for 2–3 minutes on each side until cooked through. Stir 25 g (1 oz) butter into the risotto. Scatter with chopped chives. Serve with the fish.

30 Crab Cakes with Chipotle Salsa

Serves 4

1 egg, beaten
4 tablespoons mayonnaise
2 spring onions, finely chopped
1 teaspoon Worcestershire sauce
500 g (1 lb) white crabmeat
100 g (3½ oz) dried breadcrumbs
2 tablespoons vegetable oil
salt and pepper

For the chipotle salsa

4 tomatoes, chopped
1 tablespoon finely chopped onion
1–2 teaspoons finely chopped
   chipotle chillies in adobo sauce
   or Tabasco sauce, to taste
1 tablespoon olive oil
1 lime
handful of coriander, chopped

- Mix together the egg, mayonnaise, spring onions and Worcestershire sauce. Carefully stir in the crab, trying not to break it up, then season with salt and pepper. Lightly wet your hands, then shape into 12 small crab cakes.

- Tip the breadcrumbs on to a plate, then coat the crab cakes in the crumbs. Place on a baking sheet lined with nonstick baking paper and place in the freezer for 10 minutes to firm up a little.

- Heat 1 tablespoon of the oil in a large, nonstick frying pan. Cook half the crab cakes for 3 minutes on each side until brown. Remove from the pan and keep warm in a low oven. Cook the remaining crab cakes in the same way.

- Meanwhile, for the salsa, mix together the tomatoes, onion, chillies or Tabasco and oil. Add the finely grated rind of half the lime and a good squeeze of the juice, then season. Stir through the coriander just before serving with the crab cakes.

 Crab, Pepper and Chipotle Dip

In a food processor, whizz together 1 ready-roasted red pepper, 1 teaspoon chipotle in adobo sauce or Tabasco sauce to taste, 3 tablespoons mayonnaise and 150 g (5 oz) cream cheese until smooth. Stir in 200 g (7 oz) white crabmeat. Heat gently in a small saucepan for 1–2 minutes. Serve with crackers for dunking.

 Creamy Crab and Chipotle Pasta

Cook 400 g (13 oz) dried spaghetti according to the pack instructions. Meanwhile, heat 1 tablespoon olive oil in a frying pan. Add 1 finely chopped onion and cook for 5–7 minutes until softened. Pour over 50 ml (2 fl oz) dry white wine and boil until reduced. Stir in 100 g (3½ oz) crème fraîche and 1–2 teaspoons finely chopped chipotle chillies in adobo sauce or Tabasco sauce to taste, then add 500 g (1 lb) white crabmeat. Drain the pasta and return to the pan. Toss through the crab mixture, then stir in some chopped coriander before serving.

3🌓 Smoked Haddock Soufflés

Serves 4

400 ml (14 fl oz) milk
450 g (14½ oz) smoked haddock
  fillet
75 g (3 oz) butter
2 tablespoons finely grated
  Parmesan cheese
50 g (2 oz) plain flour
75 g (3 oz) Gruyère cheese,
  grated
6 eggs, separated
2 sliced spring onions
salt and pepper

- Pour the milk over the haddock in a shallow saucepan. Simmer for 7–10 minutes until the fish flakes easily. Strain the milk through a sieve into a jug. When the fish is cool enough to handle, tear into flakes, discarding the skin and any bones.

- Meanwhile, grease 4 individual soufflé dishes well with some of the butter and dust with the Parmesan. Place on a baking sheet. Melt the remaining butter in a saucepan. Add the flour and cook for 2 minutes. Slowly whisk in the poaching milk until smooth. Bring to the boil, whisking, and when it starts to bubble and thicken, take off the heat and stir in the Gruyère and fish flakes. Stir in the egg yolks, one at a time, then leave to cool a little.

- Whisk the egg whites in a grease-free bowl until stiff and glossy. Stir one-third into the fish mixture, then carefully fold in the remaining mixture in 2 batches along with the spring onions. Spoon into the soufflé dishes. Place in a preheated oven, 200°C (400°F), Gas Mark 6, for 10–12 minutes until well risen. Serve immediately.

 Smoked Salmon Carbonara

Cook 500 g (1 lb) fresh linguine according to the pack instructions. Meanwhile, mix together 1 egg and 5 tablespoons crème fraîche. Drain the pasta and return to the pan. Add the egg mixture and toss until well combined. Toss through 150 g (5 oz) smoked salmon, cut into strips. Serve scattered with some chopped chives.

 Smoked Trout Puffs

In a food processor, whizz together 100 g (3½ oz) plain flour, 2 eggs, 300 ml (½ pint) milk and a good pinch of salt until you have a smooth batter. Grease a 12-hole muffin tray well. Break 300 g (10 oz) skinless smoked trout fillets into flakes and place a little in each hole of the tray. Divide the batter between the holes and scatter over 2 sliced spring onions. Place in a preheated oven, 220°C (425°F), Gas Mark 7, for 15 minutes or until puffed and golden.

20 Fruits de Mer with Herb Aioli

Serves 4

250 ml (8 fl oz) dry white wine

250 ml (8 fl oz) fish stock

1 bay leaf

2 raw lobster claws

4 raw crab claws

125 g (4 oz) raw small prawns, shells-on

8 langoustines

12 cleaned live clams

12 cleaned live mussels

4 oysters

For the herb aioli

2 egg yolks

squeeze of lemon juice

2 garlic cloves, crushed

200 ml (7 fl oz) olive oil

large handful of flat leaf parsley, chopped

small handful of basil, chopped

salt and pepper

• Bring the wine and stock with the bay leaf to the boil in a deep frying pan. Reduce to a simmer and add the lobster claws. Poach for 5 minutes. Remove from the pan with a slotted spoon and either keep warm or leave to cool.

• Add the crab claws, prawns and langoustines and cook for 4 minutes, then remove as before. Add the clams and mussels and cook for about 4 minutes until they have opened, discarding any that remain closed. Use the stock for making a seafood risotto or soup.

• To make the aioli, whizz together the egg yolks, lemon juice and garlic cloves in a small food processor until well combined. With the motor running, slowly start to add the oil in a thin stream until the mixture starts to thicken, then you can add the remainder a little more quickly. Season, then stir in the herbs and spoon into a serving bowl.

• Open the oysters and arrange with the rest of the seafood on a serving plate and serve with the aioli.

---

10 Fruits de Mer Rolls

Mix 6 tablespoons mayonnaise with a handful of basil and flat leaf parsley, chopped, the meat from the tail of a cooked lobster and 75 g (3 oz) white crabmeat. Split open 4 soft white rolls, spread the seafood mixture all over and top with some salad leaves and a squeeze of lemon juice.

30 Fruits de Mer with Sauce Trio

Prepare the fruits de mer and a half quantity of the herb aioli as above. For a vinegar dipping sauce, mix together 1 finely chopped shallot and 4 tablespoons red wine vinegar. For a Bloody Mary sauce, stir together 50 ml (2 fl oz) tomato ketchup, 1 chopped tomato, 3 tablespoons vodka, 2 teaspoons horseradish sauce and ½ teaspoon each Worcestershire sauce and Tabasco sauce. Serve alongside the aioli to accompany the fruits de mer.

Smoked Salmon and Beet Salad with Creamy Dressing

Serves 2

100 g (3½ oz) cooked fresh
beetroot, quartered
75 g (3 oz) beet or baby spinach
leaves
100 g (3½ oz) smoked salmon
slices
crusty brown bread, to serve
(optional)

For the creamy dressing

½ teaspoon white wine vinegar
2 tablespoons mayonnaise
2 tablespoons soured cream
1–3 teaspoons horseradish sauce
salt and pepper

- Mix together all the dressing ingredients, then season well.

- Arrange the remaining ingredients on serving plates, then drizzle over the dressing. Serve immediately with slices of crusty brown bread, if you like.

 Salmon and Beets with Creamy Dressing Heat 2 teaspoons olive oil in a nonstick frying pan. Add 2 salmon fillets, skin-side up, and cook for 3 minutes until golden. Transfer, skin-side down, to a lightly oiled baking sheet and place in a preheated oven, 200 °C (400 °F), Gas Mark 6, for about 10 minutes until the salmon is cooked through. After 5 minutes add 100 g (3½ oz) ready-cooked fresh beetroot, cut into wedges, to the baking sheet and return to the oven. Meanwhile, prepare the dressing as above. Toss with 75 g (3 oz) spinach leaves. Serve with the salmon and beets.

Salmon Carpaccio with Creamy Dressing Wrap a 200 g (7 oz) piece of salmon fillet with clingfilm, then place in the freezer for 20 minutes to firm up. Using a very sharp knife, thinly slice the fish, cutting diagonally down to create thin slivers. Arrange on serving plates. Cut 100 g (3½ oz) ready-cooked fresh beetroot into matchsticks and arrange on top. Prepare the dressing as above and drizzle over to serve.

FIS-ENTE-XEB

Chinese Banquet Sea Bass

Serves 4

750 g (1½ lb) whole sea bass, gutted and scaled

4 tablespoons Shaoxing wine

4 tablespoons soy sauce

5-cm (2-inch) piece fresh root ginger, cut into matchsticks

2 teaspoons sesame oil

2 tablespoons vegetable oil

3 spring onions, sliced

salt and pepper

- Lay the fish on a heatproof plate, then season the cavity. Pour over 1 tablespoon of the Shaoxing wine and soy sauce and place 1 tablespoon of the ginger on top. Place inside a steamer or covered wok with a rack and steam over simmering water for 15 minutes, or until the fish is cooked through. Remove the ginger and discard the cooking water.

- Heat the oils in a small saucepan. Meanwhile, arrange the spring onions and remaining ginger on top of the fish. Pour over the hot oil. Add the remaining rice wine and soy sauce to the pan and heat through briefly, then pour over the fish. Serve immediately.

Chinese Stir-Fried Sea Bass

Cut 4 x 175 g (6 oz) sea bass fillets, skin on, into pieces. Dust all over with cornflour. Heat 3 tablespoons vegetable oil in a wok and stir-fry the fish for 5 minutes until crisp and cooked through. Remove from the wok, add more oil if necessary and stir-fry 2 sliced spring onions, 1 sliced garlic clove and 1 tablespoon chopped fresh root ginger for 1–2 minutes. Pour over 1 tablespoon each soy sauce and Shaoxing wine. Return the fish to the pan, stir to coat, then serve with chopped coriander scattered on top.

Marinated Chinese Sea Bass Fillets

Mix together 2 teaspoons finely chopped fresh root ginger, 2 crushed garlic cloves, 1 thinly sliced shallot and 6 tablespoons soy sauce. Spoon over 4 x 175 g (6 oz) thin skinless sea bass fillets and leave to marinate for 10 minutes. Place each fillet on a piece of foil and spoon some of the marinade over each. Fold the foil over tightly to seal, leaving a little air around the fish. Place on a baking sheet in a preheated oven, 200°C (400°F), Gas Mark 6, for 15 minutes until the fish is just cooked through. Meanwhile, heat 1 tablespoon vegetable oil in a frying pan and gently cook 25 g (1 oz) sesame seeds until lightly browned. Spoon over the fish to serve.

30 Confit Salmon with Watercress Salad

Serves 6

6 salmon fillets, about 100 g
  (3½ oz) each
2 teaspoons salt
finely grated rind of 1 lemon
600 ml (1 pint) olive oil
12 garlic cloves
3 thyme sprigs
1 tablespoon white wine vinegar
3 tablespoons extra virgin olive oil
125 g (4 oz) watercress
salt and pepper

- Season the salmon with the salt and rub over the lemon rind. Leave to marinate for 10 minutes.

- Take a roasting tin large enough to fit the salmon fillets snugly in one layer and cover the bottom with olive oil. Place the salmon fillets, skin-side down, in the tin. Pour over the remaining olive oil, which should just cover the fish (if it doesn't quite cover it, you will need to baste a couple of times during cooking). Tuck the garlic cloves and thyme sprigs around the fish and cover with foil.

- Place in a preheated oven, 140°C (275°F), Gas Mark 1, for 15 minutes until the fish is just cooked through.

- Whisk together the vinegar and extra virgin olive oil, then season well. Toss with the watercress. Lift the salmon out of the oil and drain on kitchen paper. Serve 2 roasted garlic cloves per person with the watercress salad.

 Salmon with Watercress Pesto

Rub a little olive oil over 6 x 125 g (4 oz) salmon fillets. Cook, skin-side up, under a preheated hot grill for 5 minutes. Turn over and cook for a further 3–5 minutes until cooked through. Meanwhile, in a food processor, whizz together 100 g (3½ oz) watercress, 25 g (1 oz) toasted hazelnuts, ½ red chilli and 5 tablespoons extra virgin olive oil. Serve with the fish.

 Smoked Salmon Watercress Frittata

Heat 1 tablespoon olive oil in a nonstick frying pan. Cook 1 chopped onion for 5 minutes until softened. Whisk together 5 eggs and 2 tablespoons milk, then stir in 50 g (2 oz) roughly chopped watercress. Take the pan off the heat and pour in the egg mixture. Take 2 x 100 g (3½ oz) skinless hot-smoked salmon fillets, discard the skins and tear the flesh into chunks and stir through. Return to a low heat and cook for 10 minutes until set. Finish off under the grill to set the top, making sure you turn the handle away from the heat if not flameproof.

30 Crispy Parma Ham-Wrapped Monkfish

Serves 4

12 slices of Parma ham
625 g (1¼ lb) piece of skinless
monkfish fillet, boned and
cut into 2 fillets
2 tablespoons toasted pine nuts
3 tablespoons drained capers
4 tablespoons extra virgin olive
oil, plus extra for oiling
juice of 1 lemon
handful of flat leaf parsley,
chopped
salt and pepper

- Lay the Parma ham slices slightly overlapping on a piece of greaseproof paper. Place 1 monkfish fillet on top and lightly season. Lay the other fillet on top, the thin end facing the thick end to make a uniform-sized piece of fish. Use the greaseproof paper to roll the Parma ham around the fish. Slide on to a lightly oiled baking sheet.

- Cook under a preheated hot grill for 10 minutes, then turn over and cook for a further 7–10 minutes until the fish is cooked through and the Parma ham is crisp – to check whether the fish is cooked, insert the tip of a metal skewer into the centre, which should come out warm. Meanwhile, mix together the remaining ingredients.

- Cut the monkfish into thick pieces and serve with the sauce drizzled over.

 ### 10 Crispy Pancetta and Scallops

Heat 1 tablespoon olive oil in a large frying pan. Cut 12 slices of pancetta into thin strips. Cook for 1 minute until starting to brown. Add 12 cleaned plump scallops. Cook for 2–3 minutes on each side until browned and cooked through and the pancetta is crisp. Transfer to a serving plate. Add 50 ml (2 fl oz) water to the pan and a good squeeze of lemon juice. Boil for 1 minute. Sir in 3 tablespoons fresh green pesto and 4 tablespoons crème fraîche. Drizzle over the scallops and pancetta, then serve.

20 Crispy Parma Ham with Monkfish

Heat 2 tablespoons olive oil in a large frying pan. Cut a 400 g (13 oz) piece of skinless monkfish fillet into small medallions and cook on one side for 5 minutes until golden. Turn over and spread a little fresh green pesto over each piece of fish. Scatter over 25 g (1 oz) breadcrumbs and 15 g (½ oz) chopped pine nuts. Drizzle with a little more oil. Place the pan under a preheated hot grill, making sure you turn the pan handle away from the heat if not flameproof, and cook for a

further 3–5 minutes until golden and just cooked through. Keep warm. Heat a small, dry frying pan and cook 4 slices of Parma ham for 1–2 minutes on each side until crisp. Place the monkfish medallions on serving plates, then break the Parma ham into large pieces and scatter over the fish.

20 Chilli Crab

Serves 4

2 tablespoons vegetable oil

625 g (1¼ lb) raw crab claws

3 garlic cloves, crushed

1 tablespoon finely chopped fresh
root ginger

2–3 red chillies, deseeded
(optional) and finely chopped

200 g (7 oz) can chopped
tomatoes

1 tablespoon soy sauce

1 tablespoon Shaoxing wine

1 tablespoon soft brown sugar

2 teaspoons rice vinegar or cider
vinegar

2 teaspoons cornflour

1 tablespoon water

2 spring onions, shredded

plain rice, to serve

- Heat the oil in a large wok or frying pan. Add the crab claws and cook for about 2 minutes until bright red. Remove from the pan and set aside. Add the garlic and ginger and stir-fry for 30 seconds, then add the chillies followed by the tomatoes, soy sauce, Shaoxing wine, sugar and vinegar. Simmer for 10 minutes, adding a little water if necessary.

- Return the crab to the pan and cook for a further 5 minutes until cooked through. Mix together the cornflour and measurement water until smooth. Stir into the pan and cook for 1 minute until the sauce is slightly thickened. Scatter over the spring onions and serve with plain rice.

 Sweet and Sour Chilli Crab

Heat 2 tablespoons vegetable oil in a large wok or frying pan. Stir-fry 3 crushed garlic cloves and 1 tablespoon finely chopped fresh root ginger for 30 seconds. Add 500 g (1 lb) ready-cooked crab claws, 2 tablespoons each tomato ketchup, sweet chilli sauce and water and a pinch of sugar. Heat through. Squeeze over lime juice to taste. Scatter with chopped coriander.

 Chilli Coconut Crab Curry

Heat 1 tablespoon vegetable oil in a large wok or frying pan. Add 1 chopped onion and cook for 5 minutes until softened. Stir in 2 crushed garlic cloves, 1 tablespoon finely chopped fresh root ginger and 1–2 finely chopped red chillies and cook for a further 1 minute. Stir in 1 teaspoon each ground coriander and cumin, then add 2 lemon grass stalks and 1 kaffir lime leaf. Pour in 200 ml (7 fl oz) coconut milk and 100 ml (3½ fl oz) water. Leave to simmer for 10 minutes. Add 2 chopped tomatoes and 625 g (1¼ lb) raw crab claws and cook for 10 minutes until the crab is cooked through. Discard the lemon grass and lime leaf, then scatter with chopped coriander to serve.

30 Prawn and Leek Pot Pies

Serves 4

375 g (12 oz) ready-rolled
  puff pastry
1 egg yolk, lightly beaten
25 g (1 oz) butter
1 tablespoon olive oil
2 leeks, thinly sliced
1 tablespoon plain flour
150 ml (¼ pint) chicken stock
125 ml (4 fl oz) dry white wine
400 g (13 oz) raw peeled large
  prawns
150 ml (¼ pint) single cream
squeeze of lemon juice
salt and pepper

- Use a 250 ml (8 fl oz) ramekin to cut out 4 rounds from the puff pastry, making each one 1 cm (½ inch) larger all round than the ramekin. Place on a baking sheet and brush all over with beaten egg yolk. Bake in a preheated oven, 220°C (425°F), Gas Mark 7, for 15–20 minutes until golden and crisp.

- Meanwhile, heat the butter and oil in a saucepan. Add the leeks and a splash of water and cook for 5–7 minutes until soft. Stir in the flour, then pour over the stock and wine and leave to simmer for 7 minutes until the liquid has nearly boiled away. Add the prawns and cook for 3 minutes until cooked through, then stir in the cream and cook for a further 1–2 minutes until heated through. Season and add the lemon juice.

- Divide the mixture between 4 x 250 ml (8 fl oz) ramekins. Top with a pastry lid and serve.

---

10 Prawn Dip with Melba Toasts

Cut off the crusts of 6 thick slices of ready-sliced white bread. Carefully cut each widthways in half to make 2 thin slices. Cook under a hot grill for 1–2 minutes on each side until golden and slightly curled. Cool a little. In a small food processor, whizz together 300 g (10 oz) cream cheese and 150 g (5 oz) cooked peeled prawns to a chunky paste. Add a little lemon juice, sprinkle with paprika and serve with the toasts.

20 Upside-Down Prawn Puffs

Use a 5-cm (2-inch) cutter to cut out 4 rounds from 375 g (12 oz) ready-rolled puff pastry. Place on a baking sheet and brush all over with lightly beaten egg. Place in a preheated oven, 220°C (425°F), Gas Mark 7, for 15 minutes until golden and crisp. Meanwhile, heat 25 g (1 oz) butter and 1 tablespoon olive oil in a saucepan and cook 2 sliced spring onions for 3 minutes until softened. Stir in 50 ml (2 fl oz) dry white wine and cook until nearly boiled away. Stir through 200 g (7 oz) cooked peeled large prawns and 6 tablespoons crème fraîche and heat through. Place the pastry rounds on serving plates, spoon over the prawn mixture and scatter with chopped chives to serve.

Baked Turbot with a Buttery Tarragon Sauce

Serves 4

15 g (½ oz) butter
1.5 kg (3 lb) whole turbot, gutted
½ lemon, sliced
3 tarragon sprigs
1 bay leaf
100 ml (3½ fl oz) dry white wine
salt and pepper

For the sauce

1 shallot, finely chopped
1 tablespoon white wine vinegar
25 ml (1 fl oz) dry white wine
about 125 g (4 oz) cold butter, cut
  into cubes
handful of tarragon, chopped

- Grease a baking tray with a little of the butter, then place the fish on top, dark skin-side up. Place the lemon slices and herbs in the cavity, then pour over the wine, dot with the remaining butter and season. Loosely cover with a sheet of greaseproof or baking paper and place in a preheated oven, 200°C (400°F), Gas Mark 6, for 20–25 minutes until just cooked through.

- Meanwhile, to make the sauce, place the shallot, vinegar and wine in a saucepan and boil until reduced to 2 tablespoons. Whisking constantly, add the butter, a cube at a time, until the sauce thickens and turns creamy. Season, add a little extra butter if too sharp and stir through the tarragon.

- Serve the tarragon sauce alongside the baked turbot.

 ### Prawn Pasta with Tarragon Butter

Cook 500 g (1 lb) fresh linguine according to the pack instructions with 250 g (8 oz) raw peeled large prawns – the prawns will need about 3 minutes to cook through. Meanwhile, mix together 25 g (1 oz) each softened butter and grated Parmesan cheese, a squeeze of lemon juice and a handful of tarragon, chopped. Drain the pasta and prawns, reserving some of the cooking water. Stir through the butter with a little of the cooking water to loosen.

Grilled Cod with Tarragon Butter

Boil 4 tablespoons dry white wine in a saucepan until reduced to 1 tablespoon. Leave to cool. Mix together with 50 g (2 oz) softened butter, a handful of tarragon, chopped, and a little finely grated lemon rind. Brush a little olive oil over 4 x 150 g (5 oz) cod fillets. Cook, skin-side up, under a preheated hot grill for 5–7 minutes until browned and crisp. Turn over and cook for a further 3 minutes. Dot the butter mixture over each piece of fish and cook for 2 minutes more until the fish is cooked through and the butter melting. Serve immediately.

3 Hot-Smoked Salmon Kedgeree with Quails' Eggs

Serves 4

3 tablespoons boiling water
pinch of saffron threads
1 tablespoon vegetable oil
25 g (1 oz) butter
1 onion, finely chopped
1 garlic clove, finely chopped
1 teaspoon finely grated fresh
    root ginger
1 teaspoon mild curry powder
250 g (8 oz) basmati rice
750 ml (1¼ pints) fish or
    vegetable stock
6 quails' eggs
300 g (10 oz) hot-smoked
    salmon fillets, skinned
5 tablespoons crème fraîche
salt and pepper
chopped flat leaf parsley, to
    garnish

- Pour the measurement water over the saffron in a jug and leave to infuse. Meanwhile, heat the oil and butter in a large saucepan. Add the onion and gently cook for 5 minutes until softened. Stir in the garlic and ginger and cook for a further 1 minute. Add the curry powder followed by the rice and stir until well coated.

- Pour over the stock and saffron with its soaking liquid. Bring to the boil, then leave to simmer for 15 minutes.

- Meanwhile, boil the quails' eggs in a saucepan of boiling water for 3 minutes. Drain and cool under the cold tap, then shell and halve.

- Break the salmon into flakes and add to the rice with the egg halves. Take off the heat, cover and leave to stand for 5 minutes to warm through. Gently stir in the crème fraîche and season. Spoon on to plates and scatter with chopped parsley to serve.

 Eggs with Smoked Salmon Dippers

Bring a saucepan of water to the boil. Carefully lower in 4 hens' eggs and cook for 4 minutes for a runny yolk. Transfer the eggs to egg cups. Wrap thin strips of smoked salmon around 8 long bread sticks and use to dunk in the eggs.

 Smoked Salmon Pasta with Eggs

Infuse a pinch of saffron threads in 3 tablespoons boiling water. Meanwhile, heat 1 tablespoon olive oil in a saucepan. Cook 1 sliced shallot for 5 minutes. Pour in 150 ml (¼ pint) dry white wine and simmer for about 8 minutes until reduced. Add the saffron with its soaking liquid and 75 ml (3 fl oz) double cream and heat through. While preparing the sauce, cook 400 g (13 oz) dried spaghetti according to the pack instructions. Bring a small saucepan of water to the boil. Stir the water to create a whirlpool and crack 1 egg inside the centre. Poach for 3-4 minutes, then remove with a slotted spoon and keep warm. Repeat with a further 3 eggs. Drain the pasta and return to the pan. Toss through the saffron sauce. Serve topped with the poached eggs and scattered with strips of smoked salmon.

2 Lobster Thermidor

Serves 4

15 g (½ oz) butter
1 tablespoon olive oil
1 shallot, finely chopped
3 tablespoons dry sherry
1 teaspoon Dijon mustard
100 ml (3½ fl oz) crème fraîche
2 small ready-cooked lobsters,
   about 675 g (1 lb 5 oz) each
50 g (2 oz) Gruyère cheese,
   grated
salt

- Heat the butter and oil in a small saucepan. Add the shallot and cook for 5 minutes until softened. Pour over the sherry and cook for 2 minutes until nearly boiled away. Stir in the mustard and crème fraîche, heat through and season with salt.

- Meanwhile, using a large knife, cut the lobsters lengthways in half. Remove the meat from the tail and claws, reserving the main shell halves. Cut the lobster meat into large chunks.

- Add the lobster meat to the sauce and warm through. Carefully spoon into the tail cavities of the reserved lobster shell halves and scatter over the Gruyère. Cook under a preheated hot grill for 3–5 minutes until golden and bubbling.

1 Lobster with Thermidor Butter

Mix together 25 g (1 oz) each softened butter and grated Parmesan cheese, 1 tablespoon crème fraîche, 1 teaspoon Dijon mustard, a squeeze of lemon juice and a pinch of paprika. Use a large knife to cut 2 x 675 g (1 lb 5 oz) ready-cooked lobsters lengthways in half. Remove the meat from the claws and tuck around the tail meat. Dot 15 g (½ oz) butter all over. Cook under a preheated hot grill for 3–5 minutes until golden and bubbling, then serve.

3 Lobster in Rich Thermidor Sauce

Heat 25 g (1 oz) butter in a saucepan, stir in 25 g (1 oz) plain flour and cook for 2 minutes. Slowly whisk in 300 ml (½ pint) milk until smooth. Bring to the boil, whisking, then simmer for a few minutes until thickened. Keep warm. Meanwhile, heat 15 g (½ oz) butter in a separate saucepan. Add 1 finely chopped shallot and gently cook for about 8 minutes until very soft. Use a large knife to cut 2 x 675 g (1 lb 5 oz) ready-cooked lobsters lengthways in half. Remove the meat from the tail and claws,

reserving the main shell halves. Cut the lobster meat into large chunks. Pour 100 ml (3½ fl oz) dry white wine into the shallot pan and boil until reduced. Add to the sauce with 50 ml (2 fl oz) double cream and 2 egg yolks. Take off the heat and mix together. Add the lobster meat with a handful of tarragon, chopped, a squeeze of lemon juice and a pinch of cayenne. Return to the lobster shell halves. Scatter over 25 g (1 oz) grated Gruyère cheese. Cook under a hot grill for 5 minutes until golden brown and bubbling.

3 Whole Roasted Salmon with Lemon and Herb Tartare

Serves 4–6

3 tablespoons olive oil
1.5 kg (3 lb) thick piece of salmon,
  cut into 2 fillets
1 lemon, sliced
handful of mixed herbs, finely
  chopped
salt

For the sauce

6 tablespoons mayonnaise
2 teaspoons drained capers,
  roughly chopped
1 spring onion, chopped
1 teaspoon caster sugar
1 teaspoon wholegrain mustard
lemon juice, to taste
handful of dill, chopped

• Brush a large baking tray with a little of the oil. Place 1 salmon fillet, skin-side down, on the prepared sheet and season with a little salt. Top with the lemon slices and herbs. Season the other fillet and place on top, skin-side up.

• Tie pieces of kitchen string around the salmon to secure. Drizzle over the remaining oil. Place in a preheated oven, 220°C (425°F), Gas Mark 7, for 25 minutes, or until just cooked through.

• Meanwhile, mix together the sauce ingredients and place in a serving bowl. Serve alongside the fish with some buttered new potatoes and asparagus.

 Caper and Lemon Salmon Strips

Mix together 1 tablespoon finely chopped capers, 4 tablespoons mayonnaise and a little grated lemon rind. Cut 400 g (13 oz) skinless salmon fillet into thin strips. Place on a lightly oiled baking sheet. Thickly spread the mayonnaise on top of each strip. Scatter over 25 g (1 oz) dried breadcrumbs. Cook under a preheated hot grill for 5 minutes until cooked through.

 Salmon with Preserved Lemon

Mix together 1 teaspoon each ground cumin, paprika and finely chopped preserved lemon, a handful of coriander, chopped, and 2 tablespoons olive oil. Make slits in the skin of 4 x 150 g (5 oz) salmon fillets. Rub the spice mix all over and inside the slits. Set aside to marinate for 5–10 minutes. Heat a griddle pan until smoking hot. Cook the salmon, skin-side down, for 4–5 minutes, then turn over and cook for a further 3 minutes until cooked through. Squeeze over a little lemon juice and serve with some couscous and a tomato salad.

Pan-Fried Dover Sole with Butter and Lemon

Serves 2

75 g (3 oz) butter, plus an extra 25 g (1 oz)
2 tablespoons plain flour
2 gutted whole Dover sole, about 450 g (14½ oz) each
handful of mixed herbs including parsley, chopped
juice of ½ lemon
salt

- Heat 75 g (3 oz) butter in a small saucepan over a low heat until melted, then skim off and discard the foam on top. Pour off the clear melted butter, leaving behind and discarding the milky solids at the bottom of the pan.

- Season the flour with salt, then dust the fish all over with the seasoned flour. Heat 1 very large or 2 smaller frying pans over a medium-high heat. Add the clarified butter and cook the fish for 3 minutes. Carefully turn over and cook for a further 4 minutes, or until just cooked through. Place on serving plates.

- Wipe the pan clean with kitchen paper. Add 25 g (1 oz) butter to the pan and heat until melted. Take off the heat, stir through the herbs and drizzle over the fish with the lemon juice. Serve immediately.

 Sole Goujons with Butter and Capers

Discard the skin of 2 x 225 g (7½ oz) sole fillets and cut into 1-cm (½-inch) thick strips. Dust all over with plain flour. Heat 3 tablespoons olive oil in a frying pan and cook for 5 minutes, turning once, until just cooked through. Wipe the pan clean with kitchen paper. Add 25 g (1 oz) butter and heat until melted. Add 1 tablespoon drained capers and cook for 1 minute. Spoon over the fish with a squeeze of lemon before serving.

 Dover Sole with Butter and Wine

Season 2 x 450 g (14½ oz) gutted whole Dover sole with salt. Place on a lightly greased baking sheet. Dot over about 40 g (1½ oz) butter, drizzle over a little dry white wine and scatter over the finely grated rind of ½ lemon. Place in a preheated oven, 200°C (400°F), Gas Mark 6, for 15 minutes, or until lightly browned and just cooked through.

3⟡ Citrus Scallop Ceviche

Serves 4

½ orange

1 lime

500 g (1 lb) cleaned scallops, chopped

100 g (3½ oz) cherry tomatoes, chopped

1 tablespoon finely chopped red onion

½ red chilli, chopped

handful of coriander, chopped

2 tablespoons extra virgin olive oil

salt

- Remove the rind from the orange and lime with a zester. Squeeze the juice from the citrus fruits into a bowl and stir in the rind. Add the scallops and leave to marinate for 25 minutes.

- Toss with the tomatoes, onion, chilli and coriander, then season with salt. Pile into scallop shells or serving dishes. Drizzle over the oil and serve.

1⟡ Citrus Griddled Scallops

Toss 500 g (1 lb) cleaned scallops in 2 tablespoons vegetable oil. Heat a griddle pan until smoking hot, add the scallops and cook for 1–2 minutes on each side until just cooked through. Remove from the pan. Squeeze over the juice of ½ lime and sprinkle with 1 tablespoon orange juice, then toss with 100 g (3½ oz) chopped cherry tomatoes, 1 tablespoon finely chopped red onion, ½ chopped red chilli, a handful of coriander, chopped, and 2 tablespoons extra virgin olive oil. Season with salt before serving.

2⟡ Citrus Prawn Tostadas

Fill a large, deep saucepan one-third full with vegetable oil and heat until a cube of bread browns in 15 seconds. Deep-fry 1 corn tortilla wrap for about 1½ minutes until golden and crispy. Drain on kitchen paper. Repeat with 3 more tortillas. Leave to cool. Mix together 100 g (3½ oz) chopped cherry tomatoes, 1 tablespoon finely chopped red onion, ½ chopped red chilli, a handful of coriander, chopped, and the juice of ½ lime. Thinly slice ½ iceberg lettuce and arrange on top of the tortillas. Slice 1 avocado into thin wedges

and place on top. Scatter over the tomato mixture along with 200 g (7 oz) cooked peeled large prawns. Top with 25 g (1 oz) grated Cheddar cheese and a dollop of soured cream.

3⦿ Sea Bass Baked in a Salt Crust with Fennel Mayo

Serves 4

2 kg (4 lb) coarse sea salt
2 egg whites
1.5 kg (3 lb) whole sea bass, gutted but not scaled
½ fennel bulb, thinly sliced
1 lemon, thinly sliced
6 tablespoons mayonnaise
2 teaspoons crushed fennel seeds
1 tablespoon Pernod (optional)

- Mix together the salt and egg whites. Spread a layer of the salt mixture over the bottom of a roasting tray large enough to fit the whole fish. Place the fish on top and tuck the fennel and lemon slices inside the cavity. Completely cover with the remaining salt mixture (don't worry if the tail is still exposed). Place in a preheated oven, 200°C (400°F), Gas Mark 6, for 25 minutes until cooked through.

- Meanwhile, mix together the mayonnaise, crushed fennel seeds and Pernod, if using.

- To serve, crack the salt crust by giving it a tap with the back of a knife, then lift away. Pull the skin away from the fish, then slice into fillets and serve with the fennel mayo, some steamed potatoes and a tomato salad.

 Prawn Skewers with Chilli Salt Dip

Stone, peel and then slice a small mango into wedges. Thread on to skewers, alternating with 150 g (5 oz) cooked peeled large prawns. Mix together 2 tablespoons coarse sea salt, 1 tablespoon sugar and 1 finely chopped red chilli. Lightly dip the skewers in the salt mix before eating.

 Caribbean Salt Fishcakes

Cook 150 g (5 oz) salt fish in a saucepan of boiling water for 5 minutes. Drain and flake. Meanwhile, finely chop 3 spring onions, 1 chilli and the leaves from 1 thyme sprig. Mix with the fish, 275 g (9 oz) plain flour and 1 tablespoon baking powder. Slowly stir in 250 ml (8 fl oz) milk and 100 ml (3½ fl oz) water to make a batter just thick enough to drop off your spoon. Fill a large, deep saucepan one-third full with vegetable oil and heat until a cube of bread browns in 15 seconds. Deep-fry tablespoonfuls of the batter in batches for 2 minutes, or until golden and brown. Drain on kitchen paper, then serve.

Crispy Deep-Fried Seafood

Serves 4

50 g (2 oz) cornflour
50 g (2 oz) fine polenta
vegetable oil, for deep-frying
150 g (5 oz) cleaned baby squid,
  cut into rings
150 g (5 oz) raw peeled large
  prawns
6 cleaned plump scallops, halved
150 g (5 oz) whitebait or small
  sprats
salt and pepper
lemon wedges, to serve

- Mix together the cornflour and polenta. Place in a large freezer bag and season well. Cover a baking sheet with kitchen paper.

- Fill a large, deep saucepan one-third full with oil and heat until a cube of bread browns in 15 seconds. Add the squid to the bag and shake well until coated. Shake off the excess cornflour mixture and deep-fry for about 3 minutes, or until just golden and cooked through. Place on the prepared baking sheet and keep warm. Repeat, each in turn, with the prawns, scallops and fish. Serve with lemon wedges for squeezing over.

 Crispy-Topped Grilled Squid

Pat 200 g (7 oz) raw squid rings dry. Mix together the finely grated rind of 1 lemon, 1 teaspoon finely chopped capers and 4 tablespoons olive oil. Toss with the squid rings to coat. Arrange in a single layer on a baking sheet, then scatter over 50 g (2 oz) dried breadcrumbs and drizzle with a little more oil. Cook under a preheated hot grill for 3–5 minutes until golden and just cooked through.

 Buttermilk-Marinated Crispy Squid Pour 150 ml (¼ pint) buttermilk into a bowl. Add 300 g (10 oz) cleaned squid, cut into rings, and leave for 15 minutes to marinate. Mix together 50 g (2 oz) each cornflour and fine polenta. Place in a large freezer bag and season well. Fill a large, deep saucepan one-third full with vegetable oil and heat until a cube of bread browns in 15 seconds. Add half the squid to the bag and shake well until coated. Shake off the excess cornflour mixture and deep-fry for about 3 minutes, or until just golden. Drain on kitchen paper. Repeat with the remaining squid rings. Serve hot with lemon wedges for squeezing over.

10 Clam Linguine in Chilli Crème Fraîche Sauce

Serves 4

2 tablespoons olive oil
3 garlic cloves, sliced
½ red chilli, finely chopped
100 ml (3½ fl oz) dry white wine
1 kg (2 lb) cleaned live clams
500 g (1 lb) fresh linguine
100 g (3½ oz) crème fraîche
salt and pepper
handful of flat leaf parsley,
  chopped, to garnish

- Heat the oil in a large saucepan. Add the garlic and chilli and cook for a few seconds. Pour in the wine and bring to the boil. Add the clams, then reduce the heat, cover the pan and cook for 5 minutes until they have opened. Discard any that remain closed.

- Meanwhile, cook the pasta according to the pack instructions. Drain, reserving some of the cooking water, and return to the pan.

- Stir the pasta into the clams with the crème fraîche, adding a little of the reserved cooking water to loosen if necessary. Season, then scatter over the parsley to serve.

---

20 Clam Linguine Pasta Parcels

Cook 400 g (13 oz) dried linguine for 3 minutes less than instructed on the pack. Drain. Cook 3 crushed garlic cloves and ½ finely chopped red chilli briefly in 2 tablespoons olive oil. Add 50 ml (2 fl oz) dry white wine and 100 g (3½ oz) crème fraîche, then toss with the pasta. Divide between 4 pieces of lightly oiled foil. Top with 500 g (1 lb) cleaned live clams. Seal tightly, leaving a little air around the clams. Place on a baking sheet in a preheated oven, 200°C (400°F), Gas Mark 6, for 5–8 minutes until the clams have opened, discarding any that remain closed.

30 Spiced Clam Chowder

Heat 15 g (½ oz) butter and 1 tablespoon vegetable oil in a frying pan. Add 75 g (3 oz) lardons and cook for 3–5 minutes until golden brown. Remove from the pan. Add 1 finely chopped onion and cook for 7 minutes until softened. Stir in 1 finely chopped red chilli and return the lardons to the pan. Pour in 100 ml (3½ fl oz) dry white wine and boil for about 2 minutes until reduced. Pour in 500 ml (17 fl oz) milk and 200 ml (7 fl oz) each double cream and chicken stock and bring to the boil. Stir through 375 g (12 oz) baby potatoes, halved, and cook for 7 minutes. Add 500 g (1 lb) cleaned live clams. Cover and cook for 5 minutes until the clams have opened, discarding any that remain closed. Scatter over a handful of flat leaf parsley, chopped, to serve.